FRETBOARD ROADMAPS BASS GUITAR

THE ESSENTIAL PATTERNS THAT ALL THE PROS KNOW AND USE

The Recording
Bass—Tim Emmons
Guitars—Fred Sokolow
Sound Engineer and Other Instruments—Dennis O'Hanlon
Recorded at O'Hanlon Recording and Music Services

PLAYBACK+
Speed • Pitch • Balance • Loop

To access audio visit:
www.halleonard.com/mylibrary

2144-0297-0150-6655

ISBN 978-0-634-07901-6

Visit Hal Leonard Online at
www.halleonard.com

Contact us:
Hal Leonard
7777 West Bluemound Road
Milwaukee, WI 53213
Email: info@halleonard.com

In Europe, contact:
Hal Leonard Europe Limited
42 Wigmore Street
Marylebone, London, W1U 2RN
Email: info@halleonardeurope.com

In Australia, contact:
Hal Leonard Australia Pty. Ltd.
4 Lentara Court
Cheltenham, Victoria, 3192 Australia
Email: info@halleonard.com.au

CONTENTS

INTRODUCTION

Accomplished bass players can *ad lib* in any key—all over the fretboard. They know several different approaches to building bass lines and can choose the style that fits the tune, whether it's rock, blues, country, bluegrass, or jazz.

There are moveable patterns on the bass fretboard that make it easy to do these things. The pros are aware of these "fretboard roadmaps," even if they don't read music. If you want to jam with other players, this is essential bass knowledge.

You need the fretboard roadmaps if...

- You're starting out on the bass and you actually want to know what you're doing!

- All your bass playing sounds the same and you want some different styles and flavors from which to choose.

- You don't know how to play in every key.

- Your bass fretboard beyond the 5th fret is mysterious, uncharted territory.

- You can't automatically play a bass line for any familiar tune.

- You know a lot of "bits and pieces" on the bass, but you don't have a system that ties it all together.

Read on, and many mysteries will be explained. The pages that follow can shed light and save you a great deal of time.

Good luck,

Fred Sokolow

THE RECORDING AND THE PRACTICE TRACKS

All the bass lines, riffs, and tunes in this book are played on the accompanying recording. There are also five *Practice Tracks*. They are mixed so that the bass is on one side of your stereo and the rest of the band is on the other side.

Each track illustrates one or more roadmap concepts, such as minor pentatonics, or moveable chord-based arpeggios. You can also tune out the bass track and use the other track as backup to practice playing solos. Make sure you listen to each track before playing it on your bass.

PRELIMINARIES

Tuning

Use a tuning device or the string-to-string method described below to tune the bass:

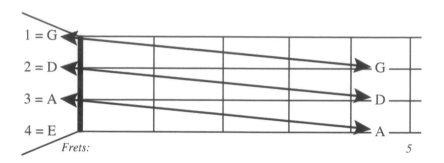

TRACK 1

As the above diagram shows, once you've tuned the open 4th/E string, you can:
1. Tune the 3rd string/A by matching it to the 4th string/5th fret,
2. Tune the 2nd string/D by matching it to the 3rd string/5th fret,
3. Tune the 1st string/G by matching it to the 2nd string/5th fret.

Unison Notes

Because of the way the bass is tuned, you can play the same note on several strings by *moving up 5 frets on a lower string*. For example, the open 1st string is G, so you can play the same G note on the 2nd string/5th fret, the 3rd string/10th fret, or the 4th string/15th fret.

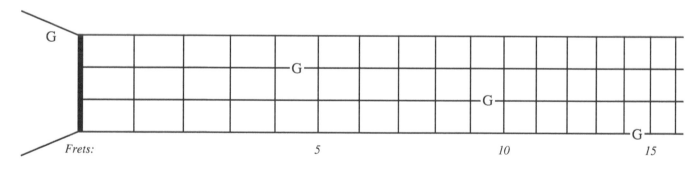

Hand Positions

See the photos below for proper right- and left-hand positioning.

HOW TO READ FRETBOARD DIAGRAMS

Each fretboard diagram is a schematic picture of the bass fretboard, as it appears when you look down at it while playing. You'll see the first fretboard diagram on the following page.

- The fourth, heaviest string (E) is at the bottom; the first, lightest string (G) is on top.

- Crucial fret numbers, such as 5, 7, 9, and 12, are indicated below the fourth string. Most electric basses have fretboard inlays at these same frets.

- Dots on the fretboard indicate where you fret the strings.

- Numbers on the fretboard indicate which finger frets the string (1=index, 2=middle, etc.).

- Letters on the fretboard are "notes" (A, B♭, C♯, etc.).

- Roman numerals (I, IV, etc.) on the fretboard are intervals, or roots of chords. Intervals and roots are explained in chapters 2 and 3.

HOW TO READ INTERVAL GRIDS

An interval grid is a picture of three or four frets of the bass fretboard. The line at the far left represents the 4th (heaviest) string; the line at the far right represents the 1st (lightest) string. The dots or letters show you where to fret (finger) the strings. The notes indicated are to be played in a sequence—not simultaneously.

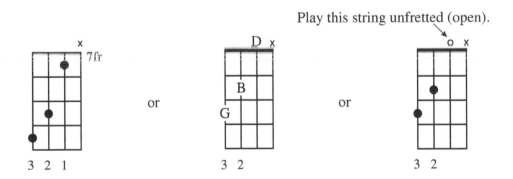

Numbers below a grid indicate the fret-hand fingering. The number to the right of the grid is a fret number. If no fret number is indicated and a thick black line is present at the top (representing the nut), the grid shows the first 3 or 4 frets of the bass.

NOTES ON THE FRETBOARD

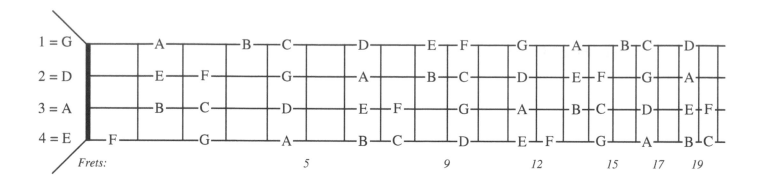

WHY? The first step in playing the bass (and understanding music) is learning where the notes are on the fretboard. The bass is an ensemble instrument, and when the guitarist or pianist says, "We're in the key of C," you better know where C is!

WHAT? **The notes get higher in pitch as you go up the alphabet and up the fretboard.**

A whole step is two frets, and a half step is one fret. Most of the notes are a whole step apart (C to D is two frets, D to E is two frets). But there are half steps in two places: from B to C is only one fret, and so is E to F.

Sharps are one fret higher: 2nd string/3rd fret = F, so 2nd string/4th fret = F♯.

Flats are one fret lower: 3rd string/2nd fret = B, so 3rd string/1st fret = B♭.

Some notes have two names. The 4th string/2nd fret is both F♯ and G♭. The name you use depends on the musical context.

HOW? **The bass is tuned E–A–D–G (from 4th to 1st string). Start by learning these notes!**

You already know some notes from the string-to-string tuning method (in the PRELIMINARIES chapter): the 4th string/5th fret = A, 3rd string/5th fret = D, and so on.

Everything starts over at the 12th fret. The open 1st string is G, so the 1st string/12th fret is also G.

Fretboard markings help. Most electric basses have fretboard inlays (dots) or marks on the neck indicating the 5th, 7th, 9th, and 12th frets. Become aware of these signposts. Eventually you'll reference them all the time: the 4th (E) string/5th fret is A, at the 7th fret it's B, and so on.

DO IT! **Learn other notes in reference to the notes you already know.** For example, the notes at the 2nd fret are a whole step (or one step of the alphabet) higher than the "open-string" (unfretted) notes, which you already know. The open 2nd string = D, so 2nd string/2nd fret = E.

Start by memorizing the 4th and 3rd strings.

- **Walk up the 4th string, naming the notes as you go.** Start with letter names; add the sharps and flats later.

- **Spot-check yourself on the 4th string.** Play random notes, out of order, naming them as you play them.

- **Learn the 3rd-string notes the same way.** Walk up the string naming the notes, and then spot-check yourself playing random notes.

Play 4th- and 2nd-string octaves to learn the 2nd-string notes. When you use the hand position shown below to play the 4th and 2nd strings simultaneously, the 2nd string note is the same note as the 4th string, only an octave (eight notes) higher. Once you have memorized the notes on the 4th string, this is a shortcut to learning the 2nd string notes.

After playing a lot of octaves, walk up the 2nd string, naming notes as you go. Keep using the 4th string as a reference point. Then spot-check yourself on the 2nd string the same way you did on the 4th string.

Play 3rd- and 1st-string octaves to learn the 1st-string notes.

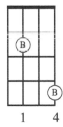

SUMMING UP—NOW YOU KNOW...

1. The location of the notes on the fretboard

2. The meaning of these musical terms:

   a) Whole Step
   b) Half Step
   c) Sharp (♯)
   d) Flat (♭)

THE MAJOR SCALE

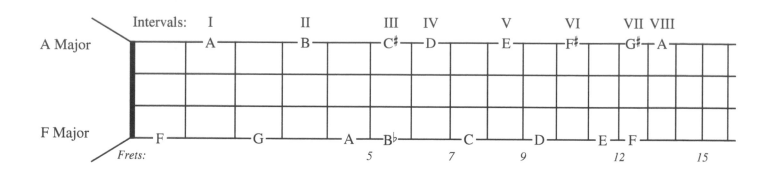

WHY? The major scale is a ruler that helps you measure distances between notes and chords. Knowing the major scale will help you understand and talk about chord construction, scales, and chord relationships.

WHAT? **The major scale is the "Do-Re-Mi" scale you have heard all your life.** Countless familiar tunes are composed of notes from this scale.

ROADMAP #2 shows two major scales: A major and F major. Walking up a single string is not the best way to play a major scale, but diagramming a scale this way makes it easy to see how the scale is constructed.

Intervals are distances between notes. The intervals of the major scale are used to describe these distances. For example, A is the third note of the F major scale, and it is four frets above F (see above). This distance is called a *major third*. On the fretboard, *a major third is always a distance of four frets* (on the same string).

The intervals of a second, third, sixth, and seventh can be major or minor. "Major" means "as in the major scale," and "minor" means flatted, or lowered one fret. For instance, A is a major third (four frets) above F, so A♭ is a minor third (three frets) above F.

An octave is the interval of eight notes. It encompasses the scale. From F to the next highest F is one octave. Notes an octave apart sound alike. They are the same note at different pitches. In other words, all Cs sound alike, as do all Ds, all Es, etc.

Music is played in keys. A key gives a piece of music a home base. A song in the "key of C" uses melody notes from the C major scale and usually ends on a C note or a C chord.

HOW? Every major scale has the same interval pattern of whole and half-steps:

C Major Scale

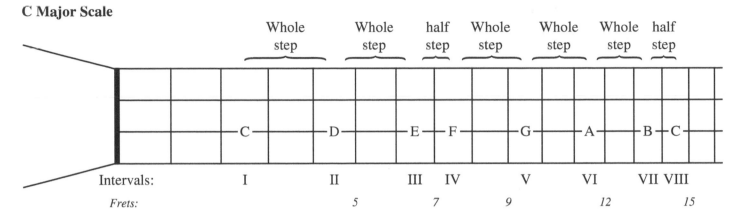

In other words, the major scale ascends by whole steps (two frets at a time) with two exceptions: there is a half step (one fret) from the third to the fourth notes and from the seventh to the eighth notes.

Every interval can be described in terms of frets. This is a helpful way for bassists to think of intervals:

— an *octave* is 12 frets. 12 frets above C is another C, an octave higher.
— a *major second* is 2 frets.
— a *major third* is 4 frets.
— a *fourth* is 5 frets.
— a *fifth* is 7 frets.
— a *major sixth* is 9 frets, or 3 frets below the octave note.
— a *major seventh* is 11 frets (or 1 fret below the octave note).
— a *minor seventh* is 10 frets (or 2 frets below the octave note).

Intervals can extend above the octave. They correspond to lower intervals:

— A *ninth* is 2 frets above the octave. It is the same note as the second, but an octave higher.
— An *eleventh* is 5 frets above the octave. It is the same note as the fourth, but an octave higher.
— A *thirteenth* is 9 frets above the octave. It is the same note as the sixth, but an octave higher.

F Major Scale

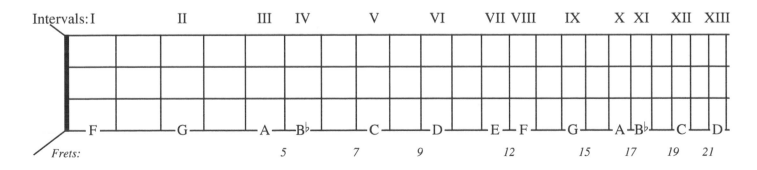

Key signatures: Every major scale (except C) contains some sharps or flats. They are identified in the *key signature* in music notation. A key signature precedes any piece of music and lets the performer know that certain notes are to be played either sharp or flat throughout the piece. Here are the most frequently used key signatures:

DO IT! **There are easier, more practical ways to play intervals on the bass** rather than counting up a certain number of frets.

• Here are the **intervals from the G major scale**, starting from the 4th string/3rd fret G note:

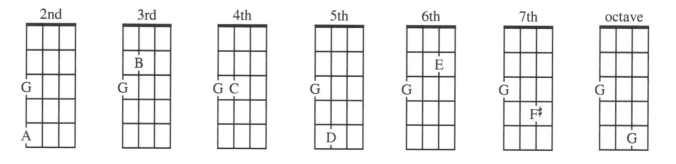

• Here are the **intervals from the C major scale**, starting from the 3rd string/3rd fret C note:

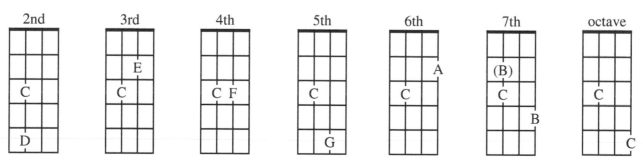

• Here are the **intervals from the F major scale**, starting from the 2nd string/3rd fret F note:

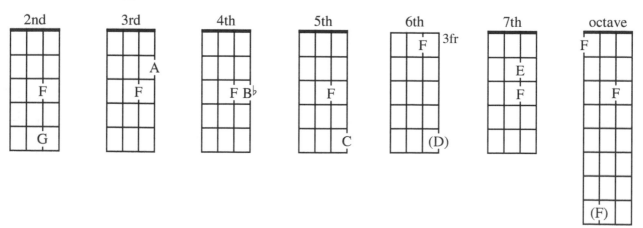

- **When a root tone is played on the second or first string, the 6th, 7th, and octaves are many frets away, so it's easier to play those intervals an octave lower, as shown in the intervals of F (previous) and intervals of B♭ (below).**

- Here are the *intervals from the B♭ major scale*, starting from the 1st string/3rd fret B♭ note:

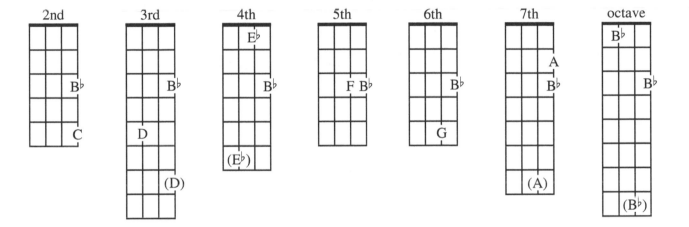

To learn the major scale intervals and the key signatures...

- Play major scales on a single string. Walk up the string, naming the notes as you go.

- Play any note and find the note that is a third higher, a fourth higher, a fifth higher, etc. Use the above "easier, more practical" way to play intervals.

SUMMING UP—NOW YOU KNOW...

1. The intervals of the major scale (whole step, whole step, etc.).

2. How to play a major scale on a single string.

3. The number of frets that make up each interval.

4. How to recognize the key signatures, and how many sharps or flats are in each key.

5. Practical ways to play intervals on the bass, starting from any string.

6. The meaning of these musical terms:

   a) Intervals
   b) Key and key signature
   c) Chord
   d) Octave

THREE MOVEABLE MAJOR CHORD SHAPES

A

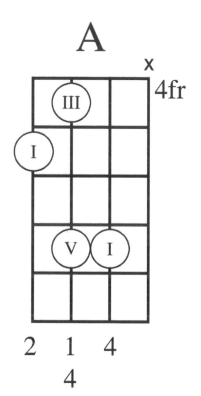

A

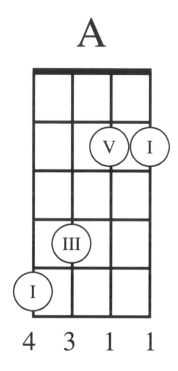

A

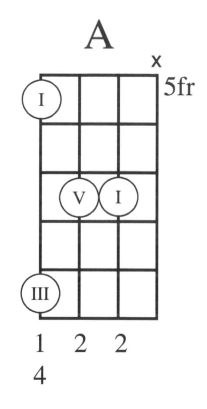

WHY? Although you seldom play chords on the bass, you often build solos and riffs around chords. Learning these major chord shapes will get you started making up bass lines.

WHAT? A "chord" is a group of three or more notes played simultaneously.

Bass lines are primarily constructed of the notes from a chord, played one note at a time.

A "root" is the note that gives a chord its name. The root of all C chords (C major, C7, C minor, C augmented, etc.) is C.

A "major chord" contains three notes: the root and the notes that are a third and a fifth above the root. In other words, a C major chord contains the 1st, 3rd, and 5th notes in the C major scale: C, E, and G.

An "arpeggio" is the notes of a chord played in succession, ascending or descending. Bass lines, riffs (repeated melodic phrases), and licks (brief melodic phrases) are often chord arpeggios.

A "moveable" chord, lick, or arpeggio can be played all over the fretboard. It contains no open (unfretted) strings. Since the moveable chord shapes have their root on the 4th string, you can move them around and identify them by the 4th string:

Roots are circled

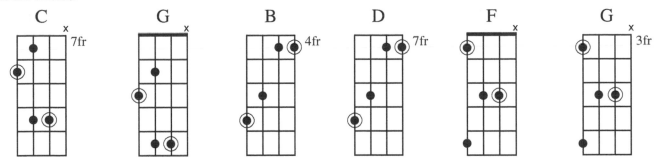

Numbers in ROADMAP #3 (below the grids) are suggested fingerings. Notice that the middle finger plays the root of one shape, the index finger plays the root of another, and the little finger plays the root of another.

Roman numerals in ROADMAP #3 are the intervals of the chord shapes.

HOW? The moveable chord shapes of **ROADMAP #3** are the basis for countless arpeggios, licks, riffs, and bass lines.

Here are some arpeggios, based on the three moveable chord shapes of **ROADMAP #3**:

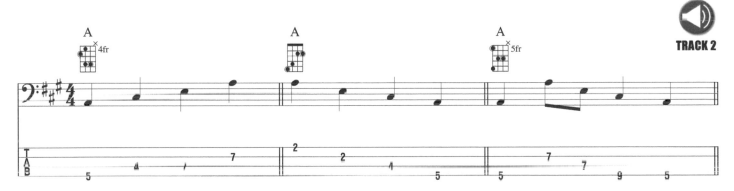

Here's how to use all three major chord shapes to create bass lines:

The repeat signs ‖: :‖ tell you to repeat the music enclosed within them.

DO IT! **Play chord arpeggios all over the fretboard, naming them as you go.** Here are some samples:

The following fretboard diagrams, along with some sample bass lines, show you how to add *"extra notes" (♭3rds, ♭5ths, ♭7ths, 6ths, and 4ths)* to your major chord shapes. These added intervals greatly expand the possibilities for bass patterns, as the samples below illustrate:

TRACK 3

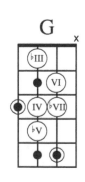

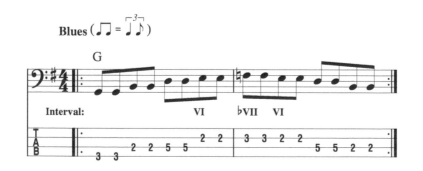

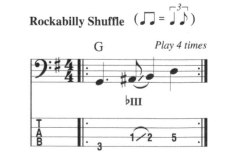

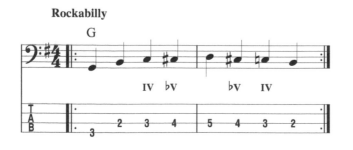

A

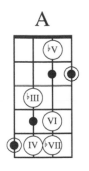

Straight-Eighths Rock

Boogie Woogie

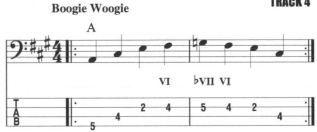

Funk

Motown

G

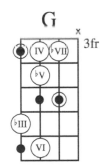

James Brown-type lick

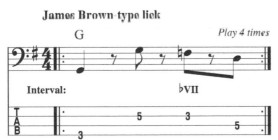

Blues Shuffle

Soul groove

Fast Motown

SUMMING UP—NOW YOU KNOW...

1. Three moveable major chord shapes with a 4th-string root.

2. Three ways to play any major chord shape.

3. How to create bass figures with each of the chord shapes.

4. How to add ♭3rds, ♭5ths, ♭7ths, 4ths, and 6ths to the three moveable chord shapes to make more interesting bass lines.

5. The meaning of these musical terms:

   a) Root
   b) Chord
   c) Major chord
   d) Arpeggio
   e) Riff
   f) Lick

MORE MOVEABLE MAJOR CHORD SHAPES

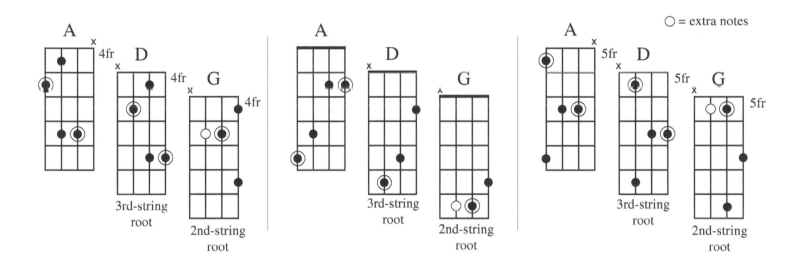

WHY? The three moveable chord shapes of **ROADMAP #3** can be moved up one string or two strings to create 3rd-string root and 2nd-string root chord shapes, respectively. In fact, most of the bass lines in the previous chapter can be played a string (or two strings) higher. This makes the three chord shapes of **ROADMAP #3** three times as useful; it also makes you a more versatile player!

WHAT? The three groups of chords in **ROADMAP #4** illustrate how to move the three chord shapes of the last chapter up one or two strings.

Move the 4th-string root chords up to the 3–2–1 string group, and they become 3rd-string root chords.

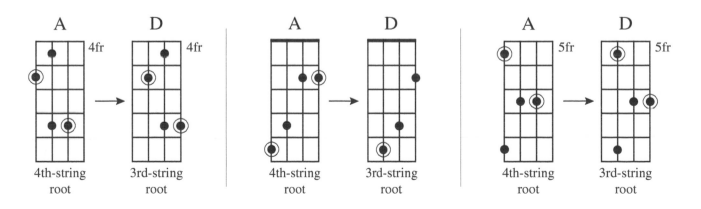

Move them up another string and they become 2nd-string root chords. You lose the highest notes in the process, so "extra," lower notes are often added to make the 2nd-string root patterns more complete and useful.

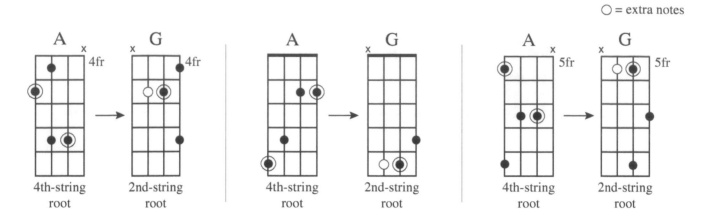

○ = extra notes

When you move up a string—e.g., from 4th string/3rd fret (G) to 3rd string/3rd fret (C)—you are moving "up a 4th." (C is a 4th above G.) This applies to chord shapes as well; when you move a G chord shape up a string, it becomes a C chord shape.

HOW?

The bass lines you played in the previous chapter are based on 4th-string root chord shapes. You can duplicate these lines using 3rd-string root chord shapes:

TRACK 6

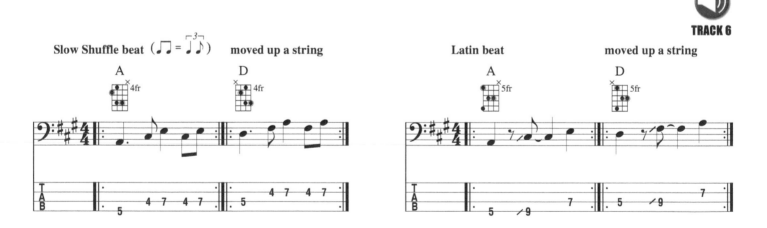

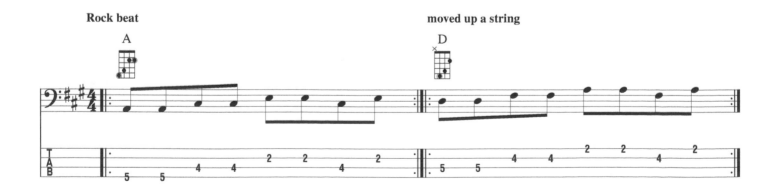

18

Some bass lines that are based on 4th-string root chord shapes can be moved up two strings, and some need to be reconfigured:

TRACK 7

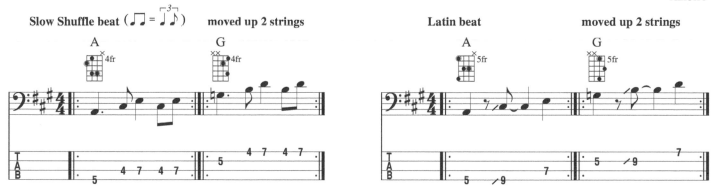

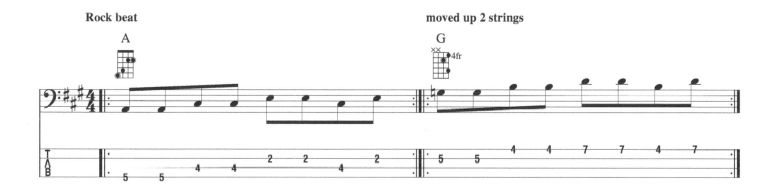

DO IT! Play 3rd-string root chord shapes all over the fretboard, naming them as you go. Here are some samples:

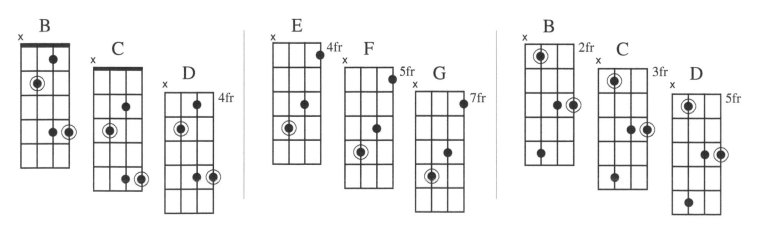

Here are some "extra notes" to help you build more interesting bass lines that are based on 3rd-string root major chord shapes and some samples of the types of bass lines that make use of the "extra notes."

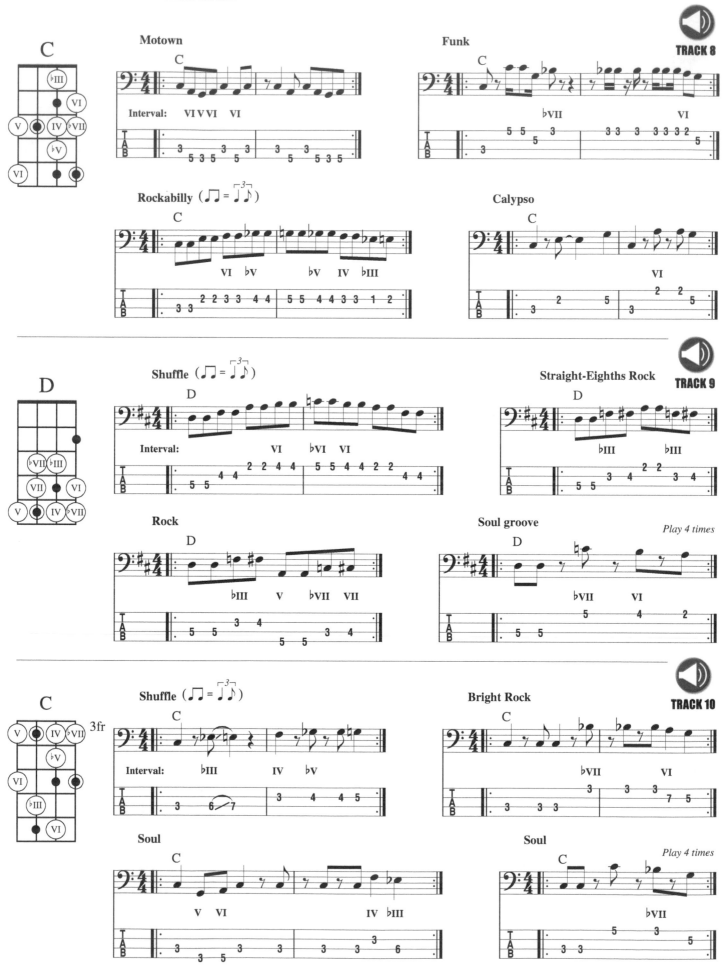

Play 2nd-string root chord shapes all over the fretboard, naming them as you go.

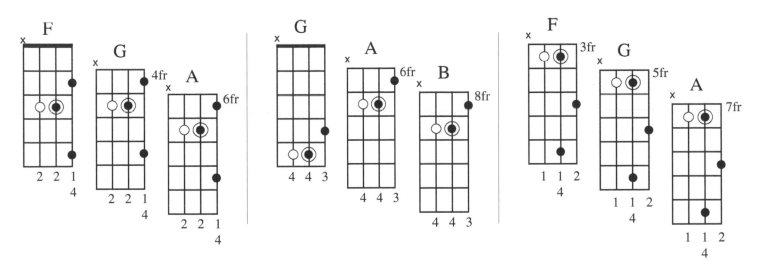

Here are some "extra notes" that help you build more interesting bass lines based on 2nd-string root major chord shapes and some bass lines that make use of them.

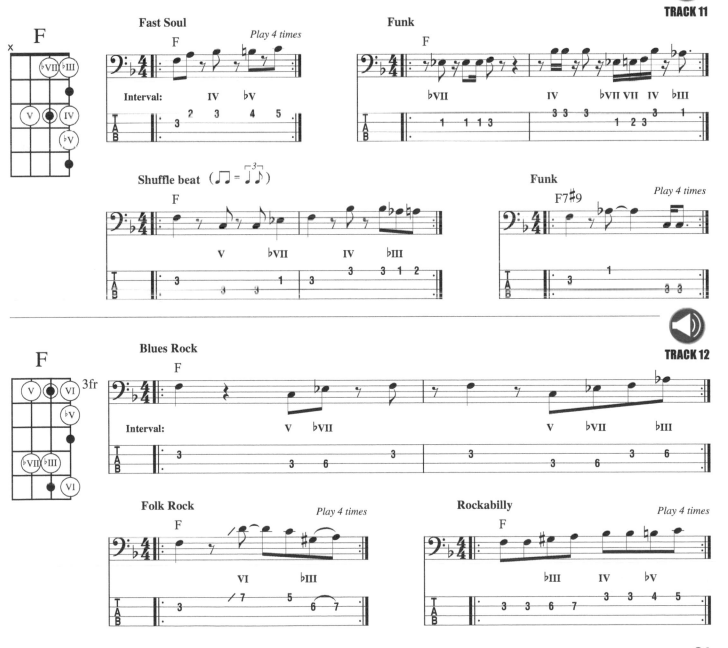

All the moveable chord shapes can be adjusted down the neck so that they include open strings.

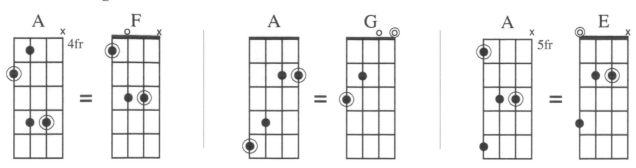

TRACK 13

The above "Latin beat" in E could be moved up a string, in order to play it in the key of A using open strings. It could also be played in D by moving it up a string:

TRACK 13 cont.

Here are some more bass lines that use open strings:

TRACK 14

50s Rock (Coasters style)

G7

70s Rock Blues

E7

SUMMING UP—NOW YOU KNOW...

1. How to alter the three moveable 4th-string root major chord shapes to create 3rd-string root chord shapes.

2. How to add ♭3rds, ♭5ths, ♭7ths, 4ths, and 6ths to the three moveable 3rd-string root chord shapes to create many types of bass lines.

3. How to alter the moveable chord shapes again to create 2nd-string root chord shapes.

4. How to add ♭3rds, ♭5ths, ♭7ths, 4ths, and 6ths to the three moveable 2nd-string root chord shapes to make more interesting bass lines.

5. How to alter the moveable chord shapes to include open strings.

THE I–IV–V "ROOT FAMILY"

G Chord Families

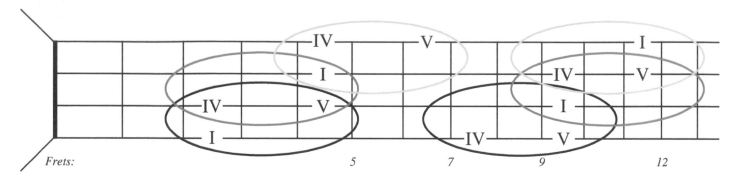

Frets: 5   7   9   12

WHY? The I–IV–V chord family is the basis for countless chord progressions in pop, rock, country, blues, and jazz. This chart shows you how to locate chord families and the roots of the I, IV, and V chords automatically, in any key, all over the fretboard.

WHAT? The Roman numerals in the chart above are the roots of the I, IV, and V chords in the key of G.

The I chord is so named because its root is the keynote—e.g., in the key of G, the G chord is the I chord.

The IV chord's root is a fourth above the keynote (a fourth above the root of the I chord). For example, C is the fourth note in the G major scale, therefore C is a fourth above G, and the C chord is the IV chord in the key of G.

The V chord's root is a fifth above the keynote. Its root is also a whole step above the root of the IV chord. D is a fifth above G (and a whole step above C), so the D chord is the V chord in the key of G.

The I, IV, and V chords form a "chord family." They are used together so frequently that in order to orient yourself to a given key, you should first locate them on the fretboard in that key.

HOW? The I–IV–V root patterns in the fretboard chart are moveable.

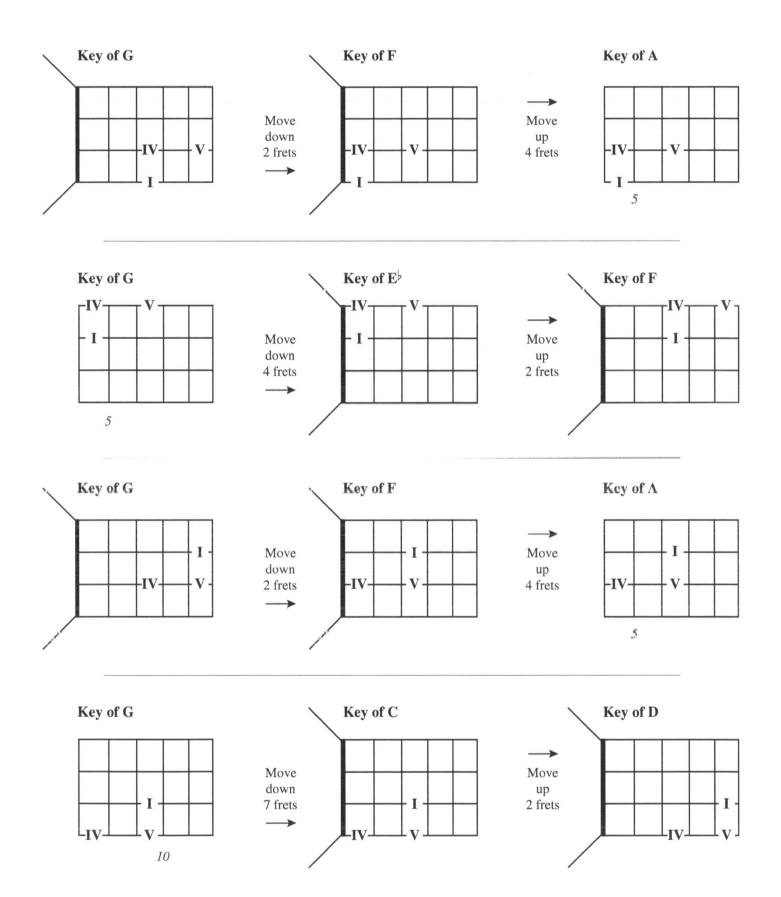

If the I is on the 4th, 3rd, or 2nd string, IV is the next highest string/same fret, and V is two frets above IV:

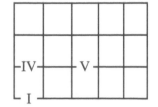

I on the 4th string

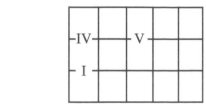

I on the 3rd string

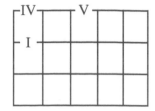

I on the 2nd string

If the I is on the 3rd, 2nd, or 1st string, V is the string below/same fret, and IV is two frets below V. So, given the previous information, you have two different ways to play the I–IV–V chord family when I is on the 3rd or 2nd string.

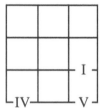 or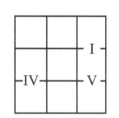

I on the 3rd string

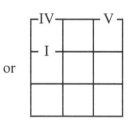 or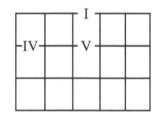

I on the 2nd string

I on the 1st string

DO IT! **Play several common I–IV–V progressions in many different keys.** For example, here is the basic rock "Louie Louie"-esque chord sequence (it is also the progression for "Wild Thing," "Good Lovin'," and "Twist and Shout"):

TRACK 17

Play the progression over and over in several keys:

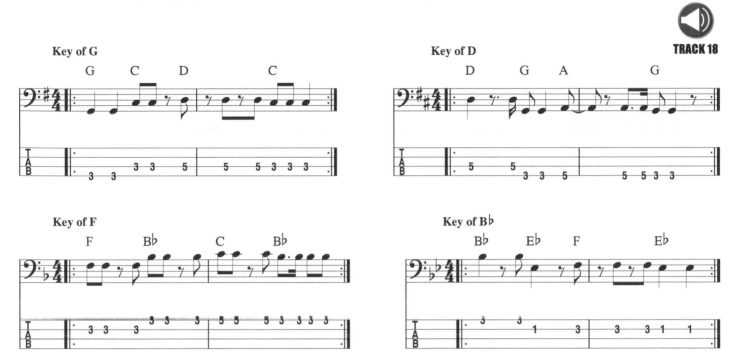

12-Bar Blues: This very important progression is the basis of countless blues, rock, country, and jazz tunes:

Play these typical, 12-bar blues/rock bass lines. Unlike the "Louie Louie"-esque progressions of Track 18, which entirely consist of root notes, these blues lines are composed of bass figures that are one or two measures long, like the bass figures in the last two chapters. In both blues samples below, a I chord figure is duplicated for the IV and V chords.

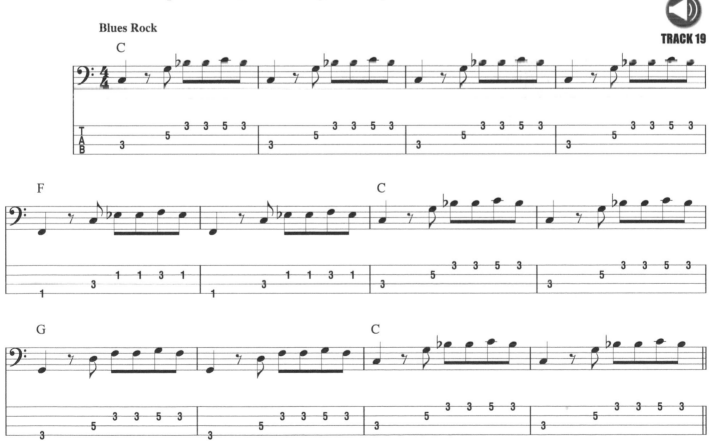

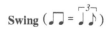

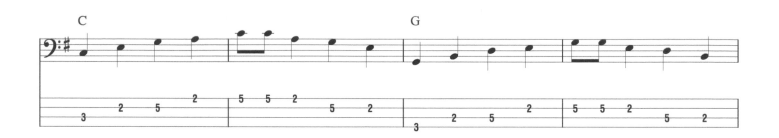

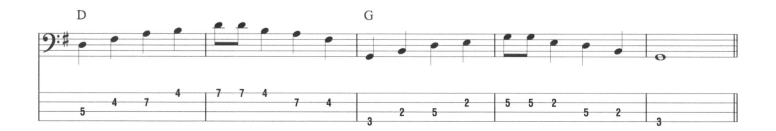

Many rock and metal tunes use the ♭III and ♭VII chords in addition to I, IV, and V. You can find the ♭III and ♭VII by relating them to the tonic (I).

— the ♭III is three frets above the I.
— the ♭VII is two frets below the I.

The fretboard diagrams below illustrate these interval relationships:

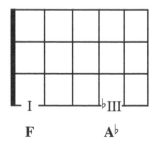

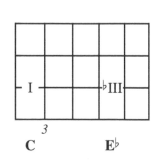

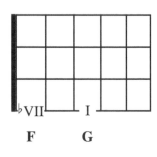

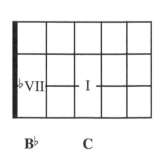

Here are some typical rock progressions that include the ♭III and ♭VII. Each is written out generically (with Roman numerals), and there is a sample bass line for each as well. Once you've played the bass line, play the same line in several different keys. This is called transposing (playing the same progression in a different key).

‖: I | ♭III IV :‖ ...as in "Purple Haze," "After Midnight," "Bang-A-Gong," "Born to Be Wild."

TRACK 20

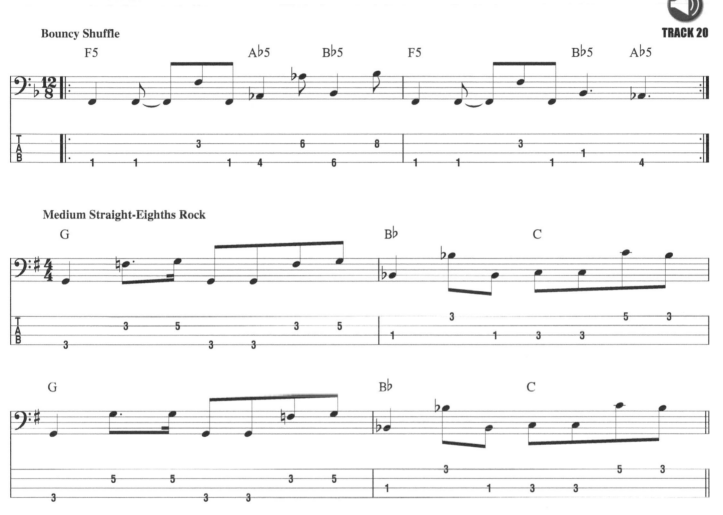

‖: I ♭VII | ♭III I :‖ ...as in the Kinks' "All Day and All of the Night."

TRACK 21

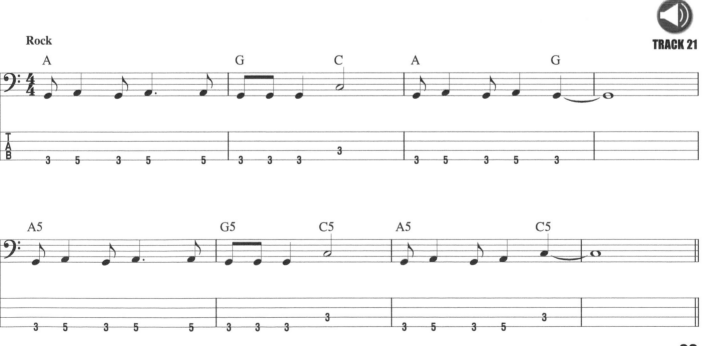

‖: I ♭VII | IV :‖ ...as in "Sweet Home Alabama" (Lynyrd Skynyrd) and "Takin' Care of Business" (Bachman-Turner Overdrive).

TRACK 22

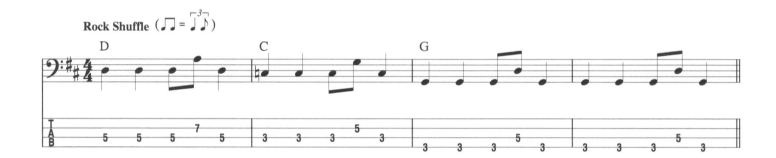

Other classic rock tunes made of I, IV, and V chords plus the ♭III and ♭VII include "Bad Medicine" (Bon Jovi), "Dude, Looks Like a Lady" (Aerosmith), "Hot Blooded" (Foreigner), and "Once Bitten Twice Shy" (Great White).

SUMMING UP—NOW YOU KNOW...

1. Three different ways to play the I–IV–V chord family—in any key.

2. Three different ways to play the 12-bar blues and the "Louie Louie" progression—in any key

3. How to find the ♭III and ♭VII and use them in progressions—in any key.

4. The meaning of these musical terms:

   a) I chord, IV chord, V chord, ♭III chord, ♭VII chord
   b) Chord Family
   c) 12-Bar Blues
   d) Transposing

THREE INVERSIONS

A Major Triads

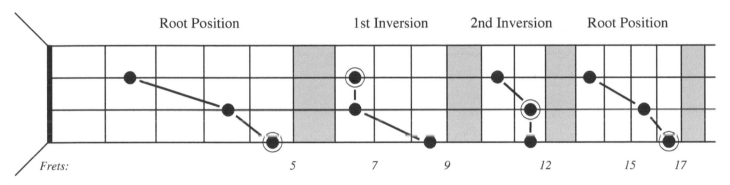

WHY? **ROADMAP #6** shows you how to put the major chord shapes of **ROADMAPS #3** and **#4** in ascending order, so you can play any given chord all over the fretboard, using three different positions. It enables you to play a bass line for any chord in the register you choose: high, middle, or low. Also, the *inversions* of **ROADMAP #6** enable you to play some very melodic and varied bass lines.

WHAT? The major chord shapes on **ROADMAP #6** are all A chords.

An "inversion" is a chord whose lowest note is not the root. Inversions are written with a slash, with the left letter designating the *chord* and the right letter designating the lowest note. A/E means "an A chord with E in the bass."

The major chords of **ROADMAP #6** are derived from the shapes in **ROADMAPS #3** and **#4**.

The *root position* is one of the 4th-string root chord shapes from **ROADMAP #3**. The root (fretted by the little finger) is the lowest note of the chord position.

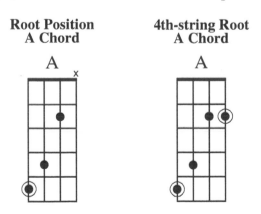

The *1st inversion* is another 4th-string root chord shape from **ROADMAP #3**. The third (fretted by the little finger) is the lowest note of the chord position:

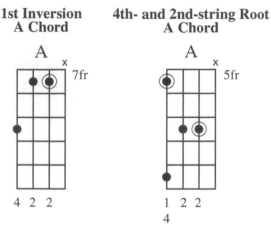

The *2nd inversion* is yet another 4th-string root position from **ROADMAP #3**, but it is *moved up a string*. The fifth (fretted by the second finger) is the lowest note of the chord position:

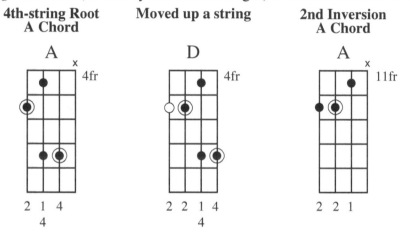

HOW?   Here's how to use **ROADMAP #6** to play all the A chord shapes:

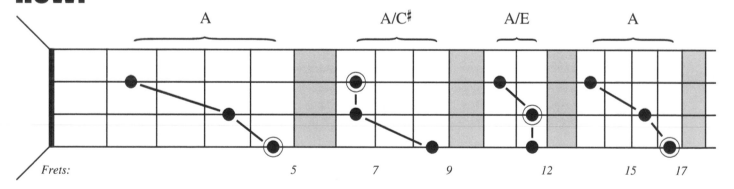

— Play the *root position* A chord shape (the lowest chord position in the diagram above).

— Skip a fret (the shaded 6th fret) and play the *1st inversion* A chord shape. Now you're playing the next higher A chord, A/C♯.

— Skip a fret (the shaded 10th fret) and play the *2nd inversion* A chord shape. This is the next higher A position, A/E.

— Skip a fret (the shaded 13th fret) and start over with the *root position* A chord shape.

— Continue the process until you run out of frets.

To memorize this roadmap, remember:

Root Position—skip 1—1st Inversion—skip 1—2nd Inversion—skip 1

Use ROADMAP #6 to play all the B chords, as shown in the fretboard diagram below.

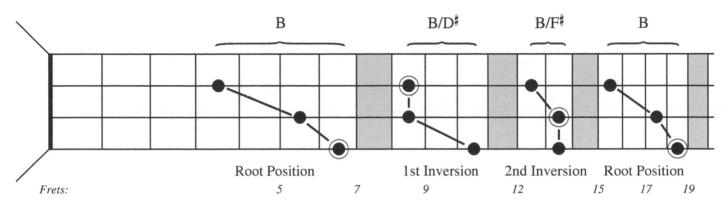

It's an endless loop that can start with any of the three positions. For example, the fretboard diagram below shows the three ascending C chord positions, starting with the *2nd inversion*.

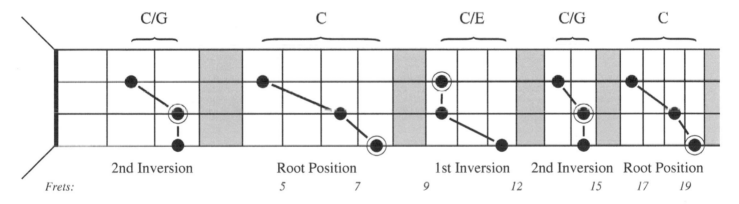

For another example, here are all the F major triads, starting with the *1st inversion:*

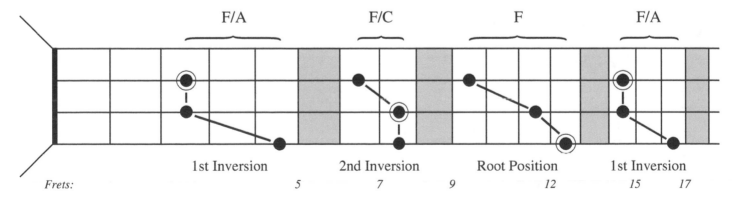

The loop can be moved up a string, which moves it "up a fourth." If you move the previous F major triad diagram up a string, you get B♭ triads (B♭ is a fourth above F).

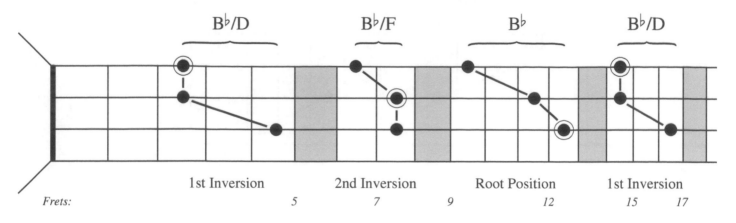

B♭/D	B♭/F	B♭	B♭/D
1st Inversion	2nd Inversion	Root Position	1st Inversion

Frets: 5   7   9   12   15   17

DO IT!

The following three bass lines make use of the three A inversions from ROADMAP #6:

TRACK 23

34

The next three bass lines are based on the three inversions of ROADMAP #6 in the key of B (as shown in a fretboard diagram in the "HOW" section):

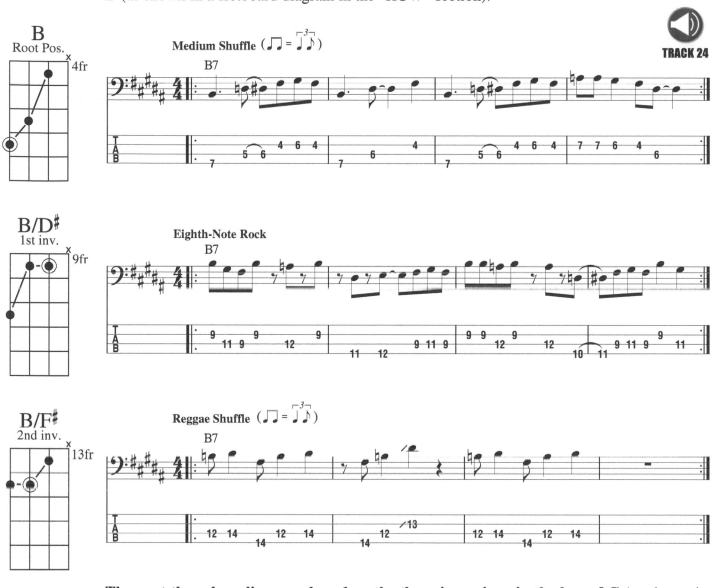

The next three bass lines are based on the three inversions in the key of C (as shown in the "HOW" section):

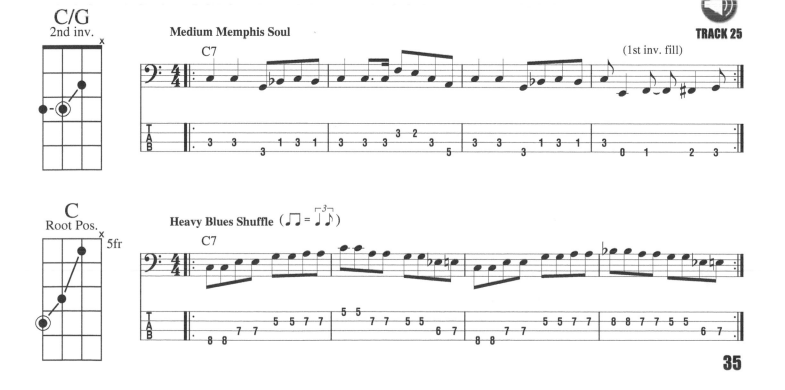

C/E
1st inv.

10fr

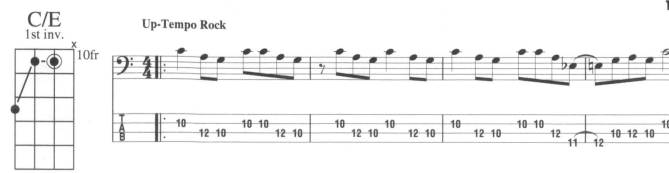

Up-Tempo Rock

Here's the previous "Up-Tempo Rock" bass line *(1st inversion)* moved down the neck to the key of F:

F/A
1st inv.

Up-Tempo Rock #2

This 3rd version of "Up-Tempo Rock" illustrates how you can move an inversion (and a bass line) **up a string and up a fourth.** The F version of "Up-Tempo Rock" has been moved up to the key of B♭:

B♭/D
1st inv.

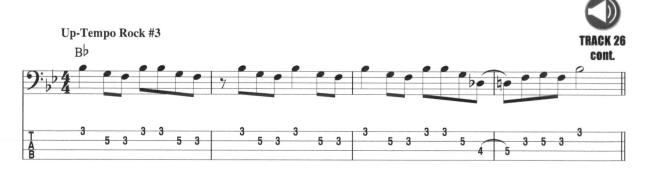

Up-Tempo Rock #3

Here's the "Medium Memphis Soul" bass line (key of C/2nd inversion) moved up a string and up a fourth, to the key of F:

F/C
2nd inv.

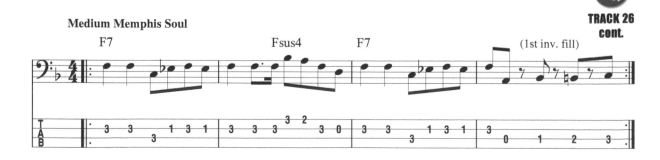

Medium Memphis Soul

36

SUMMING UP—NOW YOU KNOW...

1. How to move any chord "up the fretboard," and how to play chord shapes, bass lines, or licks in at least three positions for any key.

2. How to create melodic lines based on inversions.

3. How to play major triads with the IIIrd or Vth bottom tone.

4. The meaning of "inversion."

MOVEABLE MAJOR SCALES

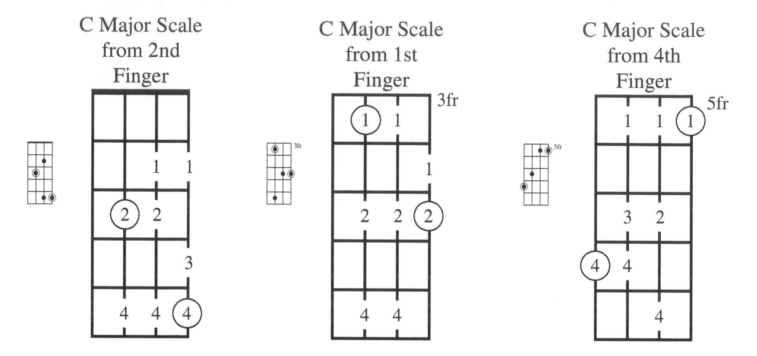

C Major Scale from 2nd Finger

C Major Scale from 1st Finger

C Major Scale from 4th Finger

WHY? The major scale is the basis for countless melodies and bass lines in tunes of many genres—rock, jazz, country, and pop. Familiarity with several major scales allows you to *ad lib* melodies or riffs. It brings you one step closer to any player's goal: to be able to play whatever you hear.

WHAT? **The numbers on the fretboard in ROADMAP #7 are left-hand fingering suggestions.** The root notes (C's) are circled.

The C major scales in ROADMAP #7 are based on the major chord positions of ROADMAPS #3 and #4. Play the appropriate major chord (the grid next to the fretboard) to get your fretting hand "in position" to play the major scale. Sometimes your left hand will move off the chord position as you play the scale, but the chord shapes are helpful frames of reference.

Here are the three C major scales of ROADMAP #7. Play each one over and over. Play the matching chord shape before playing the scale. Start each scale with its root note so you can recognize the "do-re-mi" sound you have heard all your life!

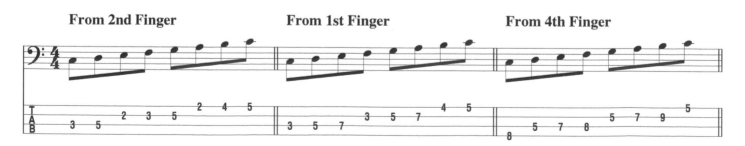

From 2nd Finger

From 1st Finger

From 4th Finger

HOW?

The scales in ROADMAP #7 are moveable. They can be played all over the fretboard:

D Major
Scale from
2nd Finger

D Major
Scale from
1st Finger

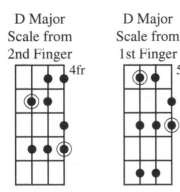

E Major
Scale from
1st Finger

E Major
Scale from
4th Finger

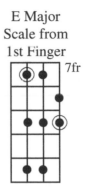
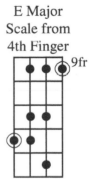

The scales in ROADMAP #7 can also be moved up or down a string to create more scale positions:

C Major
Scale from
2nd Finger

G Major
Scale from
2nd Finger

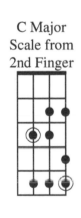
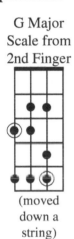

(moved
down a
string)

C Major
Scale from
1st Finger

G Major
Scale from
1st Finger

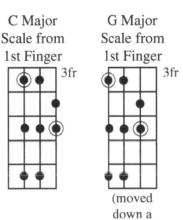

(moved
down a
string)

C Major
Scale from
4th Finger

F Major
Scale from
4th Finger

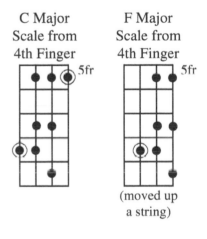

(moved up
a string)

DO IT!

Play different scales over and over, in several places on the fretboard. For example, play three different F major scales, three different E♭ scales, B♭ scales, etc.

Once you are familiar with a scale pattern, use it to play melodies. This is great ear training. Start with simple, familiar tunes, such as nursery rhymes:

C

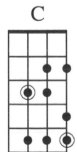

C Major Scale

Mary Had a Little Lamb

Twinkle Twinkle Little Star

Some bass lines are very scalar. The next three bass lines ("1950s Rock") are examples of a common chord progression found in doo-wop tunes like "Oh, Donna," "(Why Must I Be) A Teenager in Love," and countless other songs of that era. The bass lines make use of three different C major scales:

The "Rockabilly Shuffle" and "Medium Blues Rock" examples are also based on major scales:

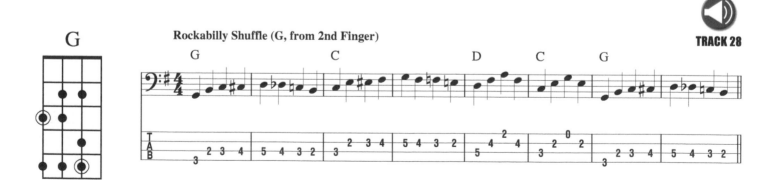

C

Medium Blues Rock (C, from 4th Finger)

"Country Two-Beat" is based on the 4th finger/C major scale pattern moved up a string. Because it starts at the 3rd string/3rd fret, it makes use of open strings:

Country Two-Beat (C, from 4th Finger)

The following key-of-F version of "Country Two-Beat" is the same as the previous C version, but it's moved up a string.

Country Two-Beat (F, from 4th Finger)

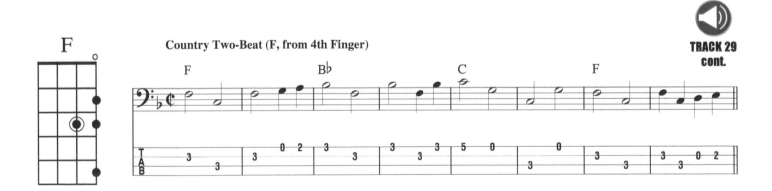

Here's another "Country Two-Beat"—three versions of it, in three keys—that has several "bass runs." These brief, major-scale based licks that connect one chord to another are characteristic of country and bluegrass music. This "Two-Beat" is played in C, moved down a string to the key of G, and finally moved back up a string and down three frets to the key of A, where open strings are used.

TRACK 30

Country Two-Beat (C, from 2nd Finger)

Country Two-Beat (G, from 2nd Finger)

Country Two-Beat (A, from 2nd Finger)

SUMMING UP—NOW YOU KNOW...

1. How to play three moveable major scales for each key.

2. How to play melodies and bass lines in all keys in two or three registers.

3. How to make double use out of the moveable major scales by moving them up or down a string.

MOVEABLE MAJOR PENTATONIC SCALES

Key of C:

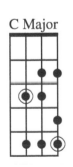 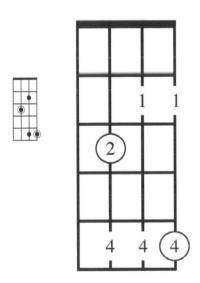   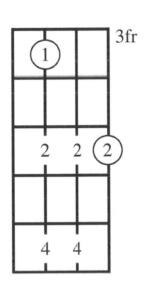 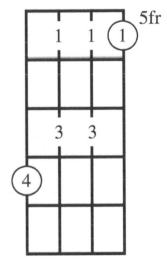

WHY? The versatile major pentatonic scales can help you play bass lines in rock, country, jazz, blues, and pop tunes. They are especially useful for "walking bass" lines and boogie grooves.

WHAT? The major pentatonic (five-tone) scale consists of the 1st, 2nd, 3rd, 5th, and 6th notes of the major scale. In the key of C, that's C, D, E, G, and A. Hum the "My Girl" riff to remember the major pentatonic sound.

Major pentatonic scales are simplified major scales. Compare major scale positions of **ROADMAP #7** to the major pentatonic scales:

C Major | C Major Pentatonic | C Major | C Major Pentatonic | C Major | C Major Pentatonic

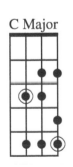  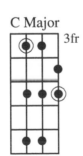 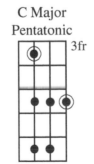 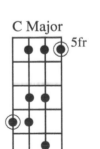 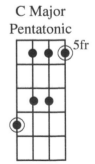

The three scales in **ROADMAP #8** are C scales. The roots are circled. The numbers are fingering suggestions.

HOW?

ROADMAP #8 shows how to play most pentatonic bass lines three different ways, using three different positions. For example, there are three ways to play this R&B pattern:

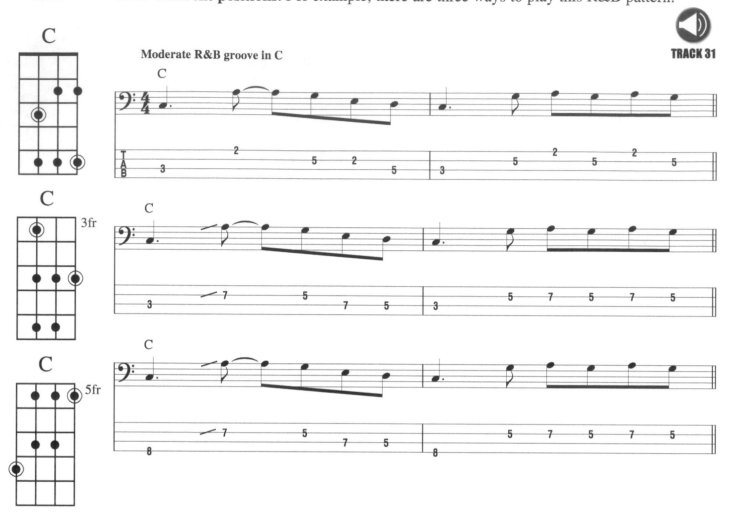

You can play the scale patterns lower on the fretboard and use open strings:

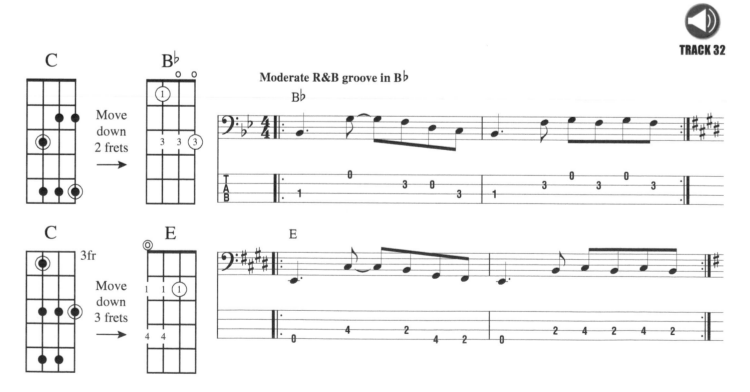

You can use the scale patterns of **ROADMAP #8** to play in any key. The roots of the scale are circled, so start any pattern in whatever key you like. For example, to play in the key of E, the diagram shifts like this:

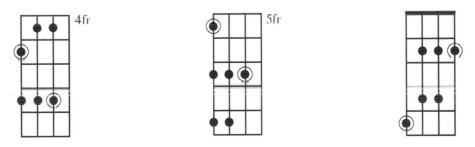

Sometimes it's convenient to shift the first two patterns of **ROADMAP #8** down a string, so they start on the fourth string. In the following A major pentatonic scales, the first two patterns are shifted down to the fourth string.

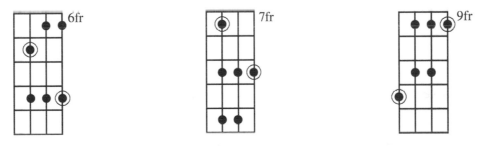

The 3rd-string root scales are useful for bass lines that go below the root note:

Many boogie-bass lines are built on the major pentatonic scale:

A

Boogie Shuffle in A

TRACK 34

Bb

Boogie/Rock in Bb

The flatted third and flatted seventh are often added in boogie bass lines:

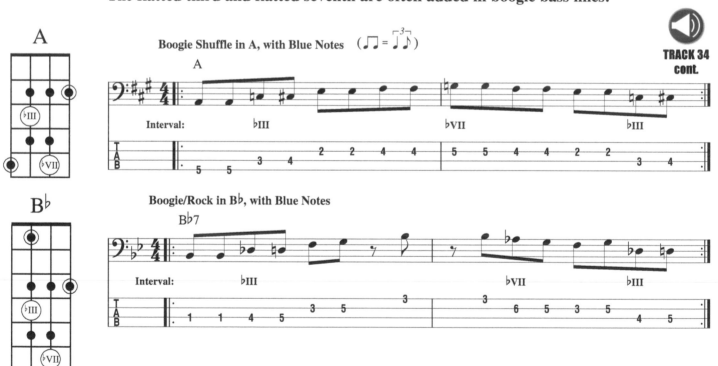

A

Boogie Shuffle in A, with Blue Notes

TRACK 34
cont.

Bb

Boogie/Rock in Bb, with Blue Notes

Here's a two-octave lick that illustrates one way to connect two major pentatonic scales:

F   F   Rock

TRACK 35

DO IT! Here are some bass lines from a variety of musical genres, all built on major pentatonics:

TRACK 36

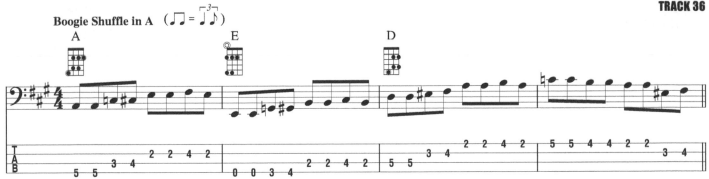

TRACK 37

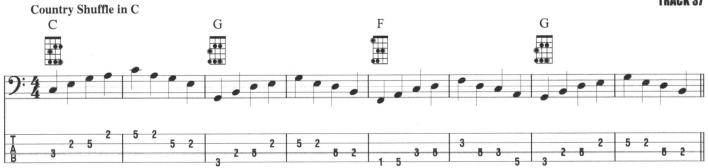

TRACK 38

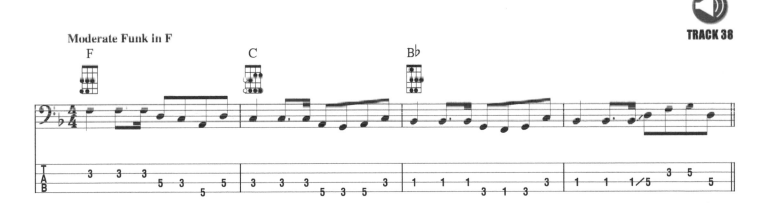

SUMMING UP—NOW YOU KNOW...

1. Which notes make up a major pentatonic scale.

2. How to play three major pentatonic scales, ascending the neck, in any key.

3. How to use the major pentatonic scales to build bass lines.

4. How to shift the scales down to include open strings.

MOVEABLE MINOR SCALES

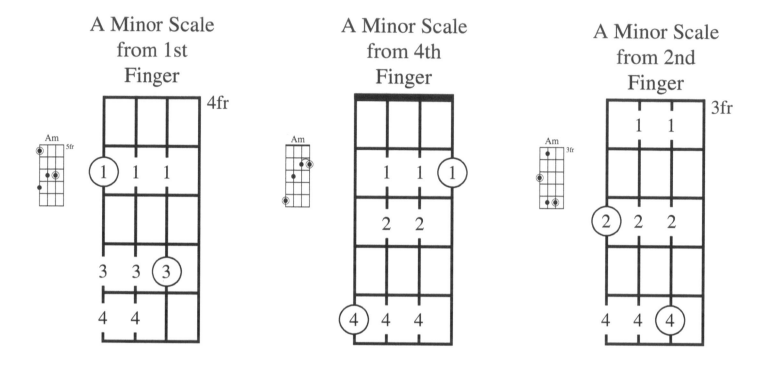

WHY? The scales and chord shapes in **ROADMAP #9** help you build bass lines and riffs for songs in minor keys.

WHAT? **The numbers on the fretboard in ROADMAP #9 are left-hand fingering suggestions.** The root notes (A's) are circled.

A minor chord is the same as a major chord (1–3–5), but the third is flatted (lowered by a half step).

The A minor scales in ROADMAP #9 resemble the major scales of ROADMAP #7, but the 3rds, 6ths, and 7ths are flatted. Those flatted intervals define the minor scale.

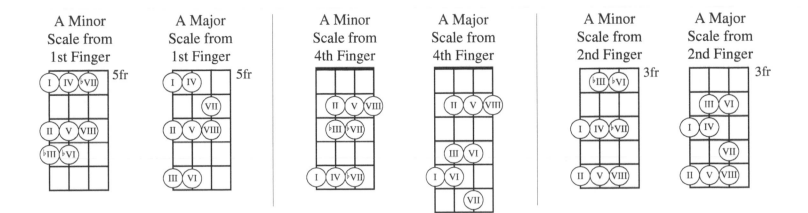

Play the appropriate minor chord (the grid next to each scale in **ROADMAP #9**) to get your fretting hand "in position" to play a minor scale.

Here are the three A minor scales of **ROADMAP #9.** Play each one over and over.

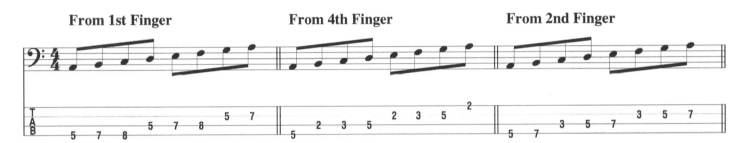

HOW? The scales in **ROADMAP #9** are moveable. They can be played all over the fretboard. If moved low enough, they may include open strings:

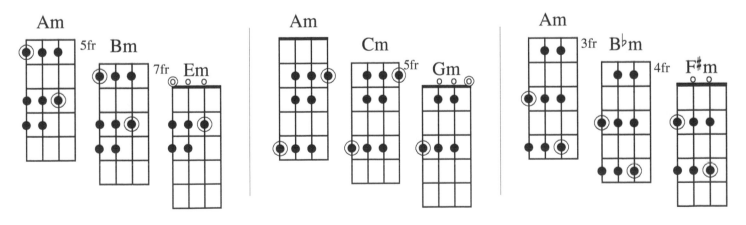

The scales in **ROADMAP #9** can also be moved up or down a string to create more scale positions:

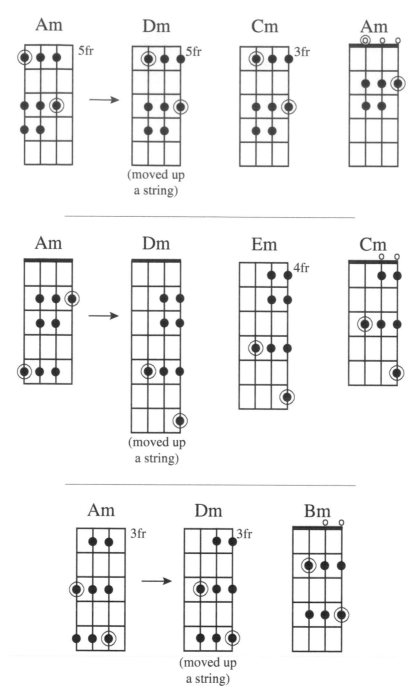

DO IT! **Play different scales over and over,** in several places on the fretboard. For example, play three different G minor scales, three different D minor scales, etc.

G minor

D minor

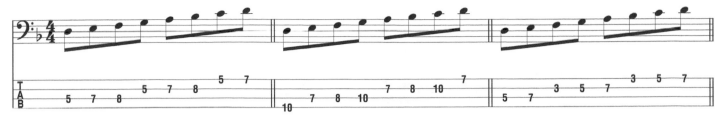

Here are some lines that are based on minor scales:

TRACK 39

TRACK 40

SUMMING UP—NOW YOU KNOW...

1. How to play three moveable minor scales for each key.

2. How to play bass lines in all minor keys in two or three registers.

3. How to make double use out of the moveable minor scales by moving them up a string.

MOVEABLE MINOR PENTATONIC SCALES

Key of A Minor:

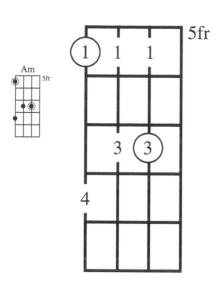

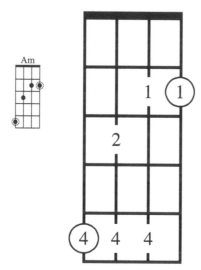

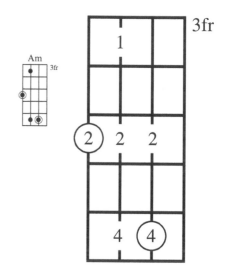

WHY? Minor pentatonic scales are sometimes called *blues scales*, and they're useful when you're building bluesy bass lines or playing bluesy riffs or licks. Since blues is the foundation of jazz and rock and is also an important element in country, pop, old standards, and show music, every bass player needs to know the minor pentatonic scales.

WHAT? The three scale patterns of **ROADMAP #10** are A minor pentatonic scales. The root notes are circled. The numbers indicate suggested fingering.

Minor pentatonic scales are simplified minor scales. The five notes of the minor pentatonic scale are the 1st, ♭3rd, 4th, 5th, and ♭7th notes of your key. The A minor pentatonic blues scale consists of A (I), C (♭III), D (IV), E (V), and G (♭VII).

Compare the pentatonic and minor scales:

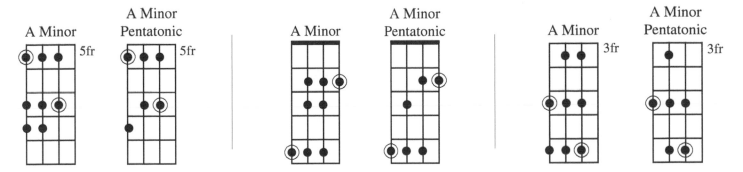

Sometimes the flatted fifth is added. This creates a *blues scale*.

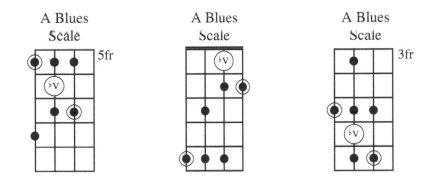

A minor pentatonic bass line can be played several different ways, using the three positions:

Minor pentatonics are not just for minor keys! A minor pentatonic bass line can be played over a minor or major key blues or rock tune if the song's melody is based on the blues scale, rather than the major scale.

HOW? You can use the scale patterns of **ROADMAP #10** to play in any key. The roots of the scales are circled, so start any pattern in whatever key you like. For example, to play in the key of C, the diagram shifts like this:

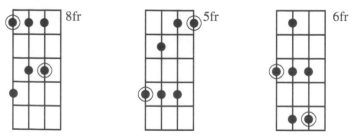

If you shift the patterns up, so that the root is on the third string, you can play bass lines that go below the root note:

Moderate Rock in D

TRACK 42

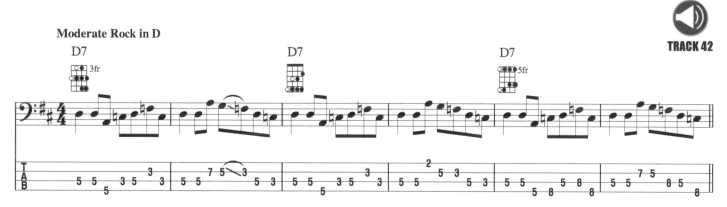

To play in E or A, you can move the scale patterns down the fretboard and use open strings. The E scale below is the same as the first pattern of **ROADMAP #10** moved down five frets. The A scale in measure 3 is the same as the E scale, moved up a string.

Slow Rock in A Minor

TRACK 43

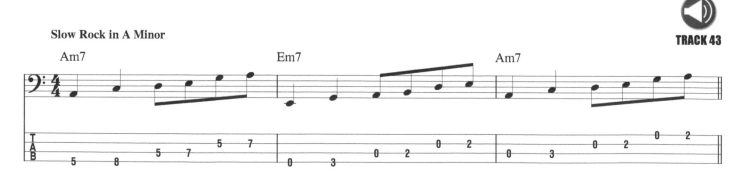

DO IT!

Here are some minor pentatonic and blues scale bass lines:

TRACK 44

Last 4 bars of a 12-bar Blues Shuffle in G

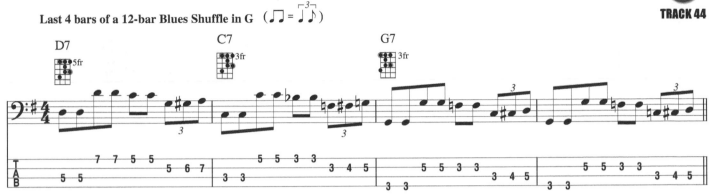

TRACK 45

Moderate Blues/Rock in E♭

TRACK 46

Funk groove in A

SUMMING UP—NOW YOU KNOW...

1. Which notes make up the minor pentatonic and blues scales.

2. How to play three minor pentatonic and blues scales in any key.

3. How to use the minor pentatonic and blues scales to build bass lines.

4. How to shift the scales down to include open strings.

THE CIRCLE-OF-FIFTHS

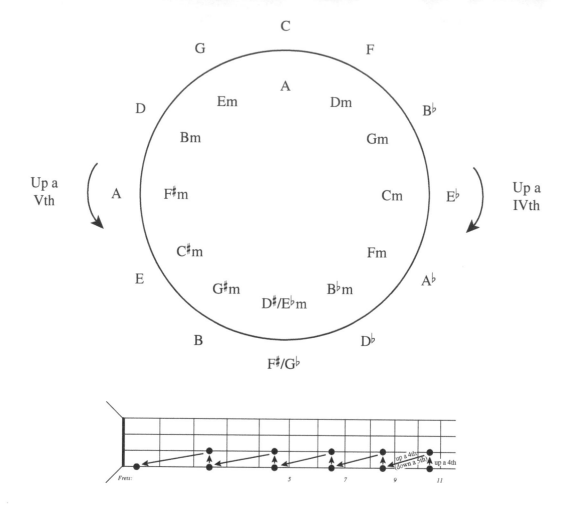

WHY? An understanding of the circle-of-fifths, combined with this root pattern diagram, makes it easy to play several frequently-used chord progressions—automatically, in any key.

WHAT? The circle-of-fifths (also called the "circle-of-fourths") arranges the twelve musical tones so that a step counter-clockwise takes you up a fifth, and a step clockwise takes you up a fourth.

— Counter-clockwise: G is a fifth above C, D is a fifth above G, etc.

— Clockwise: F is a fourth above C, B♭ is a fourth above F, etc.

— This arrangement makes chord families visual on the circle: If C is your I chord, F (IV) is next to it on the right, and G (V) is next to it on the left.

Relative minors are inside the circle (e.g., Am is the relative minor of C). The relative minor chord's root is a minor third (three frets) below its relative major. The two chords contain many of the same notes and are closely related.

If I, IV, and V chords make up the immediate family, their relative minors are the extended family. They are often used in common chord progressions. Thus, in the key of C: C (I), F (IV), and G (V) are an immediate chord family, and the relative minors are Am (relative minor to C), Dm (relative to F), and Em (relative to G).

Transposing means changing a song's key. The circle diagram is a useful tool that can help you transpose. If you find a tune written in a songbook in E♭ and you want to play it in the key of C, notice the distance between E♭ and C on the circle of fifths: C is three steps counter-clockwise from E♭. To transpose from E♭ to C, move every chord in the tune three steps counter-clockwise. A♭ becomes F, Cm becomes Am, etc.

HOW? **Circle-of-fifths progressions:** Thousands of songs, from century-old ragtime to contemporary rock, are based on circle-of-fifths-type motion. In a circle-of-fifths progression, you leave the I chord and come back by clockwise motion, going up by fourths until you are "home" at the I chord. For instance, in the key of C:

TRACK 47

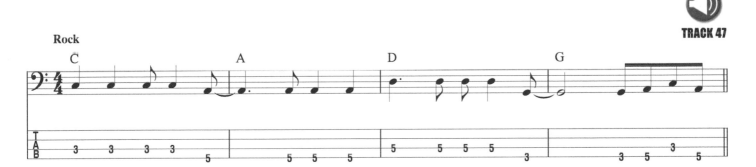

— In the above *I–VI–II–V progression*, you jump to the VI chord (A), then go clockwise to the II chord (D). This is going up a fourth; D is a fourth above A. Next you play V (G), which is a step clockwise on the circle and is a fourth from D (G is the fourth note in the D scale). Go another step clockwise (up another fourth) to I (C) and you're home.

Every chord is a fourth above the previous chord—that's circle-of-fifths motion. But in relation to C, you played I–VI–II–V.

— In another circle-of-fifths progression, the VI and II chords are minor (written: vi and ii). In the key of C:

TRACK 48

This *I–vi–ii–V progression* is so common it has many names among pros: standard changes, dimestore progression, ice cream changes, rhythm changes (a reference to Gershwin's "I Got Rhythm" that features the progression), etc. It is the basis for countless 1930s and 40s tunes ("Blue Moon," "Heart and Soul," "I Got Rhythm"), 50s and 60s rock ballads ("Oh Donna," "Silhouettes," "You Send Me," "Sincerely," "All I Have to Do Is Dream," "Stand By Me"), and more recent pop tunes ("Every Time You Go Away," "Morning Train [Nine to Five]," "Everybody Has a Hungry Heart").

In many I–vi–ii–V progressions, IV is substituted for ii, which changes the progression to I–vi–IV–V, or, in the key of C: C–Am–F–G7. It's a subtle change, because IV and ii are very similar chords; ii is the relative minor to IV (e.g., in the key of C, Dm is the relative minor to F).

The second half of the previous progression, *ii–V–I,* is the basis for many tunes and is also a *turnaround* (a one- or two-bar phrase at the end of a verse or chorus that sets up a repeat of the section). "You're So Fine," "El Paso," and "Satin Doll" are based mostly on ii–V–I.

TRACK 49

III–VI–II–V–I progressions go a step further back on the circle:

TRACK 50

This is the same chord progression as the "I Got Rhythm" bridge, which occurs in many tunes. It is also the basis for many standards like "All of Me" and "Please Don't Talk About Me When I'm Gone." Sometimes the III, VI, or II is minor.

— **Still other tunes cycle back even further, to the VII chord.** In the key of C:

TRACK 51

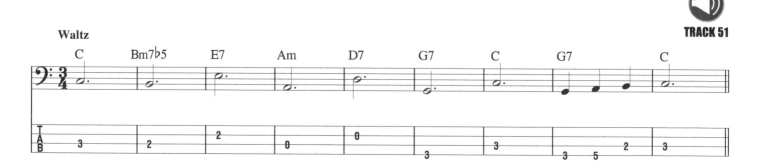

"Mister Sandman" and "Red Roses for a Blue Lady" are two examples of VII–III–VI–II–V–I progressions.

Circle-of-fifths/fourths movement on the fretboard follows a zig-zag root pattern.

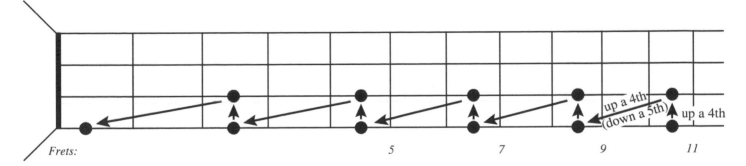

— Starting with a 4th-string note (the root of a chord), you go up a fourth (one step clock-wise on the circle) by going up a string to the 3rd string/same fret (e.g., from D, 4th string/10th fret, to G, 3rd string/10th fret).

— Starting with a 3rd-string root note you get to the root of the IV chord (one step clock-wise on the circle) by going down a string to the 4th string/two frets lower (e.g., from G, 3rd string/10th fret to C, 4th string/8th fret).

— Thus, you play circle-of-fifths progressions when you follow the zig-zag chart above, in which each note is the root of a chord. For example, you could play a VII–III–VI–II–V–I progression in D♭ like this, starting from the VII chord:

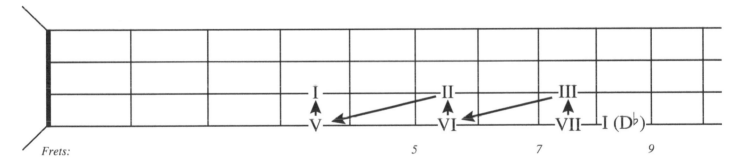

DO IT! Just as the I–IV–V root patterns of **ROADMAP #5** help you locate chord families automatically on the fretboard, so does **ROADMAP #11** help you play circle-of-fifths chord progressions.

— **ii–V–I:** Play the following ii–V–I phrases in the key of B♭. The root of the I chord is on the 3rd string. Notice that the zig-zag pattern can be moved up a string to the 3rd and 2nd strings:

TRACK 52

Hip-Hop

— Here's that last ii–V–I phrase in B♭ with a 4th-string root/I chord:

Relative minors can be found automatically.

Root of I chord on the 4th string—key of A

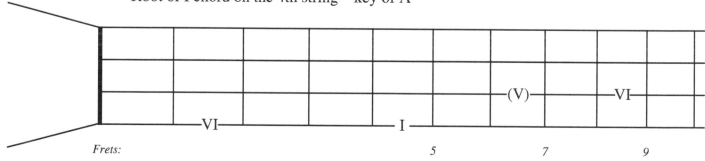

Root of I chord on the 3rd string—key of D

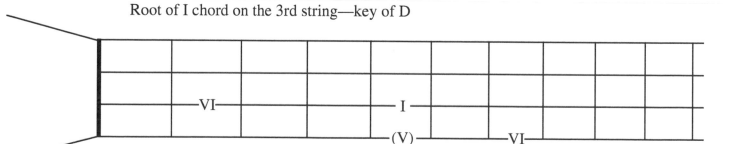

As the fretboard root-pattern charts above indicate, there are two ways to find the root of a relative minor. Both ways work for a 4th- or a 3rd-string/root I chord:

— The root of the relative minor is three frets below the root of the I chord.

— The root of the relative minor is two frets above the root of the V chord (VI is two frets above V).

Here's a bass line that goes from a major chord to its relative minor. The first time around the progression you get to the relative minor by going down three frets from the I chord. The second time you go up two frets from the V chord to get to the relative minor.

TRACK 54

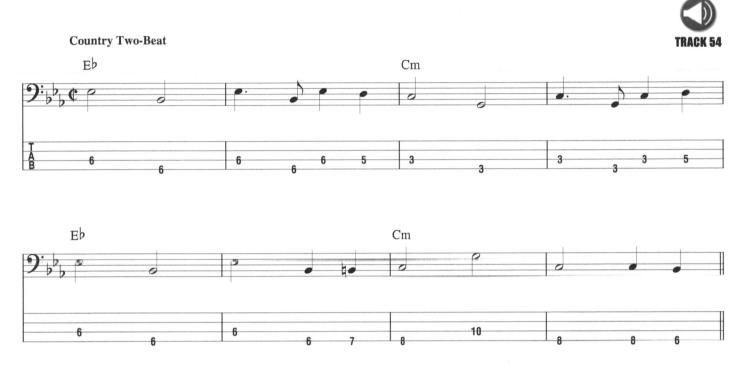

I–vi–ii–V: To play this popular progression, you jump from the root of the I chord to the root of the vi chord and zig-zag back to I. Here are some sample bass lines:

TRACK 55

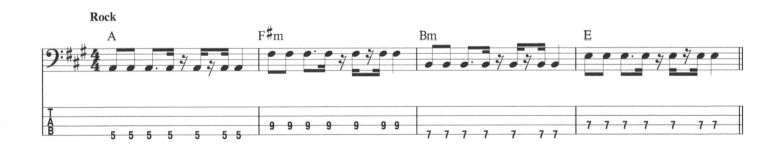

III–VI–II–V–I and VII–III–VI–II–V–I: Do some serious zig-zagging and play these sample progressions:

TRACK 56

TRACK 57

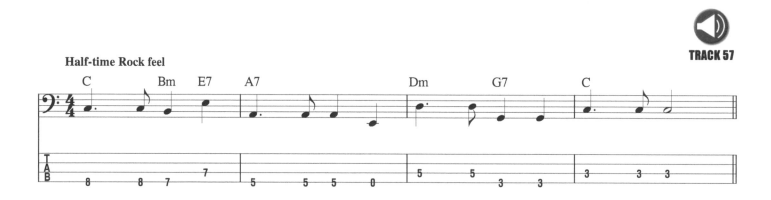

SUMMING UP—NOW YOU KNOW...

1. How to play several circle-of-fifths progressions in any key using the "zig-zag" method: ii–V–I, I–vi–ii–V, III–VI–II–V–I, and more.

2. How to locate relative minor chord/roots on the fretboard.

3. How to transpose.

4. The meaning of these musical terms:

   a) Circle-of-fifths/fourths
   b) Relative Minor
   c) Relative Major
   d) Transposing

FIVE- AND SIX-STRING BASS CONVERSIONS

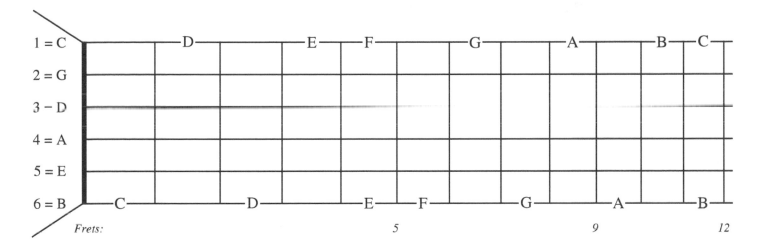

1 = C		D		E	F		G		A		B	C
2 = G												
3 = D												
4 = A												
5 = E												
6 = B	C		D		E	F		G		A		B

Frets: 5   9   12

WHY? Five- and six-string electric basses are being used more and more. These instruments offer more range with less horizontal changes of position; you can play more than two octaves without shifting up the neck. They also allow you to play both higher and lower notes than one can play on the four-string bass.

WHAT? **The fifth string of the five-string bass is a low B note. The six-string bass features a low B string and a high C string.** The added low notes are especially useful, and the higher string has a guitar-like timbre.

If you have a five-string bass, leave out the high C-string notes when you play the exercises and examples in this chapter.

To learn how to use the extra strings, extend the fretboard roadmap patterns you have already learned. They can all be converted to include the low B and high C strings.

HOW? **The six-string bass, like the four-string bass, is tuned to ascending fourths.** The low sixth string is B; the next (fifth) string is a fourth higher (E); the next (fourth) string is a fourth above E (A), and so on.

Because of this tuning, you can make use of the high C and low B strings by moving the Roadmaps you've already learned in this book (scales and chord positions) up or down a string.

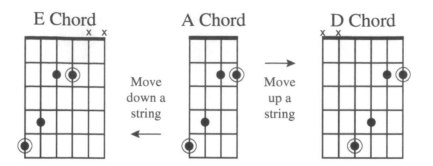

You can also enlarge the given chord and scale positions by extending them to include the new strings.

- Here's how to extend one of the three moveable major chord shapes of **ROADMAP #3** to include the B and C strings. The extended E major arpeggio starts with the first finger on E at the B string/5th fret:

Notice the fingering patterns:
   1. Play the first E with the first finger on the sixth (B) string/5th fret.
   2. Play the octave E with the second finger at the A string/7th fret.
   3. Play the second octave E with the fourth finger at the G string/9th fret.

- **With this fingering, you can play two octaves, or two chord patterns, without changing positions or shifting up the neck:**
   — The first finger plays the root note.
   — The second finger plays the octave note and starts the next pattern.

- **Here's the same E major arpeggio starting with the second finger pattern.** Once again, you play two patterns without changing position. You start with the second finger on the sixth string/5th fret, and the first finger plays the second octave E on the C string.

Here's the third E major chord arpeggio, starting with the fourth finger on the B string/5th fret.

1. Play the octave E with the first finger at the D string/2nd fret.
2. Play the second octave E with the second finger on the C string/4th fret.

• **If you extend ROADMAP #7 to include the B and C strings in moveable major scales, the same sequence of finger patterns will occur, allowing you to play two octaves without shifting up the neck:**

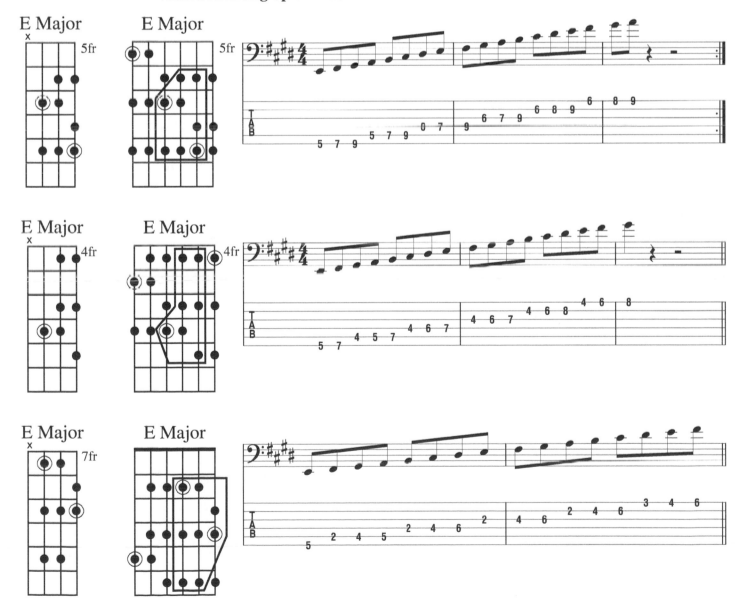

DO IT! **Play the following two-octave, F major pentatonic lick.** Start at the B string/6th fret. Play it from either the second or fourth finger.

Rock (F, from 2nd Finger)

(F, from 4th Finger)

Play the moveable minor pentatonic scale patterns of ROADMAP #10. The first D minor pentatonic scale starts on the B string/3rd fret. Fret this D note with the first finger.

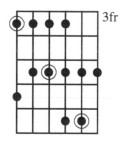
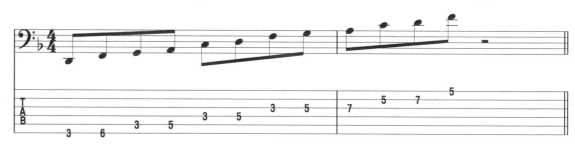

The next extended D minor pentatonic scale starts with the second finger.

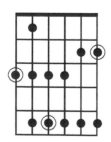
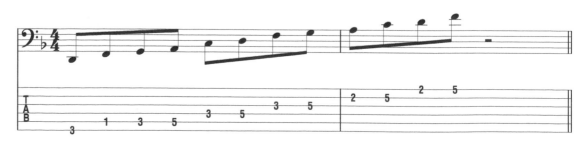

Play the extended E minor pentatonic scale. It starts with the fourth finger on the B string/ 5th fret.

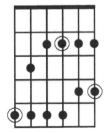
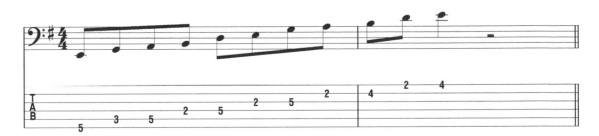

Play the following E minor pentatonic lick.
— It starts with the fourth finger on the B string/5th fret.
— The octave E is played on the D string/2nd fret with the first finger.
— The second octave E is played at the C string/4th fret.
— If you don't have a C string, shift to frets 7 and 9 on the G string for the high D and E, and play the last G on the open string.

TRACK 59

SUMMING UP—NOW YOU KNOW...

1. How to tune the sixth/B and first/C strings.

2. How to extend the various roadmaps to include these two strings.

USING THE PRACTICE TRACKS

The roadmaps illuminate many approaches to constructing bass lines, including:

- chord arpeggios

- major scales

- major pentatonic scales

- minor scales

- minor pentatonic scales

For the five practice tracks, the bass is separated from the rest of the band—it's on one side of your stereo. You can tune it out and use the band as backup, trying out any bass lines you like. You can also imitate the bass; here are the underlying ideas behind each bass track:

TRACK 60

Practice Track 1: "Rock Groove" has a common I–IV–V progression in G, with some relative minor chords in the bridge. The bass line is built on chord arpeggios. Here's the progression:

> *Play 4 times*
> Verse: ‖: D | C | G | G :‖
>
> Bridge: | Em | Em | Bm | Bm | Em | Em | Am Bm | C D ‖

TRACK 61

Practice Track 2: "Blues Rock," in the key of A, has a funky feel, and the bass lines are built on the A minor pentatonic scale. It's a 12-bar blues:

> ‖ A7 | A7 | A7 | A7 | D9 | D9 | A7 | A7 | E9 | D9 | A7 | A7 E9 ‖

Practice Track 3: "Twelve-Bar Shuffle Swing" has a rockabilly/swing feel. The bass line is built on major pentatonics. The second time around the progression, blue notes are added to the bass line. Chromatics are added the third time around. The key is B♭:

TRACK 62

> ‖ B♭7 | B♭7 | B♭7 | B♭7 | E♭9 | E♭9 | B♭7 | B♭7 | F9 | E♭9 | B♭7 | B♭7 F9 ‖

Practice Track 4: "Motown Groove" has a fast rock/soul feel, and the bass line is built on major scales. Here's the key-of-E progression:

TRACK 63

> ‖ E | A | E | A | F♯m7 | B7 | F♯m7 | B7 | E | E/G♯ | A | A♯°7 | E | A | E | A |
>
> | F♯m7 | B7 | E | D | E | D ‖

Practice Track 5: "Jazz Ballad" is built on circle-of-fifths chord movement, and the bass makes use of chord-based licks and major scales. Here's the progression (it's in the key of C):

TRACK 64

> ‖ Cmaj7 B7 | E9 A7 | Dm7 G7 | C C♯°7 Dm7 G7 | C B7 | Emaj7 | Am7 D7 |
>
> | Dm7 G7 ‖ Cmaj7 B7 | E9 A7 | Dm7 G7 | Em7♭5 A7 | Dm7 Dm7♭5 |
>
> | Em7 A7 | Dm7 G7 | C6 ‖

LISTENING SUGGESTIONS

Every aspiring musician listens to the masters of their favorite musical genre to pick up ideas, style, timing, nuances, and licks. Here are some listening suggestions: listen and play along with the best!

Classic Rock: Paul McCartney (the Beatles), John Paul Jones (Led Zeppelin), Leland Sklar (James Taylor, the Section), Phil Lesh (Grateful Dead), John Entwistle (the Who), Hutch Hutchinson (Bonnie Raitt), Bill Wyman (Rolling Stones), Steve Harris (Iron Maiden), Chris Squire (Yes).

Contemporary Rock: Les Claypool (Primus), Mike Gordon (Phish), Krist Novoselic (Nirvana), and listen to the bassists with these groups: Radiohead, Pearl Jam, Metallica, Smashing Pumpkins.

Country: Listen to the bassists with any contemporary country artists, as well as these "classic country" artists: Merle Haggard, George Jones, Buck Owens, Willie Nelson.

Jazz: Jaco Pastorius (solo/Weather Report), Jimmy Haslip (solo/Yellowjackets), John Patitucci (solo/Chick Corea), Victor Wooten (solo/Bela Fleck and the Flecktones), Anthony Jackson (solo/Michel Camilo), Todd Johnson (solo/Ron Eschete trio), Jeff Berlin (solo/Bill Bruford), Abraham Laboriel (Fourplay).

Rap/Hip Hop: Mike Elizondo (Dr. Dre/Eminem), Pino Palladino (D'Angelo and many groups).

Funk/R&B: James Jamerson (most Motown recordings 1962–73), Donald "Duck" Dunn (Booker T & the MGs, Otis Redding, Sam and Dave, Wilson Pickett, Blues Brothers), Marcus Miller (solo/Miles Davis), Paul Jackson (Herbie Hancock), Rocco Prestia (Tower of Power), Bootsy Collins (solo/Parliament-Funkadelic), Larry Graham (pioneer of slap-bass, Sly & the Family Stone), Melvin Davis (Chaka Khan), Verdine White (Earth, Wind & Fire).

Reggae: "Family Man" Barrett (Bob Marley & the Wailers), Robbie Shakespeare (Sly and Robbie, Rita Marley), Jackie Jackson (Jimmy Cliff).

World Beat: Listen to the bassists with artists like Sunny Ade, Fela Kuti, Yasoun D'our, any West African "High Life" or Zouk music.

BASS NOTATION LEGEND

Bass music can be notated two different ways: on a *musical staff*, and in *tablature*.

THE MUSICAL STAFF shows pitches and rhythms and is divided by bar lines into measures. Pitches are named after the first seven letters of the alphabet.

TABLATURE graphically represents the bass fingerboard. Each horizontal line represents a string, and each number represents a fret.

Notes:

3rd string, open   2nd string, 2nd fret   1st & 2nd strings open, played together

HAMMER-ON: Strike the first (lower) note with one finger, then sound the higher note (on the same string) with another finger by fretting it without picking.

PULL-OFF: Place both fingers on the notes to be sounded. Strike the first note and without picking, pull the finger off to sound the second (lower) note.

LEGATO SLIDE: Strike the first note and then slide the same fret-hand finger up or down to the second note. The second note is not struck.

SHIFT SLIDE: Same as legato slide, except the second note is struck.

TRILL: Very rapidly alternate between the notes indicated by continuously hammering on and pulling off.

TREMOLO PICKING: The note is picked as rapidly and continuously as possible.

VIBRATO: The string is vibrated by rapidly bending and releasing the note with the fretting hand.

SHAKE: Using one finger, rapidly alternate between two notes on one string by sliding either a half-step above or below.

NATURAL HARMONIC: Strike the note while the fret hand lightly touches the string directly over the fret indicated.

MUFFLED STRINGS: A percussive sound is produced by laying the fret hand across the string(s) without depressing them and striking them with the pick hand.

BEND: Strike the note and bend up the interval shown.

BEND AND RELEASE: Strike the note and bend up as indicated, then release back to the original note. Only the first note is struck.

RIGHT-HAND TAP: Hammer ("tap") the fret indicated with the "pick-hand" index or middle finger and pull off to the note fretted by the fret hand.

LEFT-HAND TAP: Hammer ("tap") the fret indicated with the "fret-hand" index or middle finger.

SLAP: Strike ("slap") string with right-hand thumb.

POP: Snap ("pop") string with right-hand index or middle finger.

ADDITIONAL MUSICAL DEFINITIONS

 (accent)   • Accentuate note (play it louder)

 (accent)   • Accentuate note with great intensity

 (staccato)   • Play the note short

   • Downstroke

∨   • Upstroke

D.S. al Coda   • Go back to the sign (𝄋), then play until the measure marked "***To Coda***," then skip to the section labelled "**Coda**."

D.C. al Fine   • Go back to the beginning of the song and play until the measure marked "***Fine***" (end).

Bass Fig.   • Label used to recall a recurring pattern.

Fill   • Label used to identify a brief pattern which is to be inserted into the arrangement.

tacet   • Instrument is silent (drops out).

• Repeat measures between signs.

1. 2.   • When a repeated section has different endings, play the first ending only the first time and the second ending only the second time.

NOTE: Tablature numbers in parentheses mean:
1. The note is being sustained over a system (note in standard notation is tied), or
2. The note is sustained, but a new articulation (such as a hammer-on, pull-off, slide or vibrato begins), or
3. The note is a barely audible "ghost" note (note in standard notation is also in parentheses).

ABOUT THE AUTHORS

FRED SOKOLOW is a versatile "musicians' musician." Besides fronting his own jazz, bluegrass, and rock bands, Fred has toured with Bobbie Gentry, Jim Stafford, Tom Paxton, Ian Whitcomb, Jody Stecher, and the Limeliters, playing guitar, banjo, mandolin, and Dobro. His playing has been heard on numerous TV shows, commercials, and feature films, including the recent Bogdanovitch movie *The Cat's Meow*.

Sokolow has written over a hundred stringed instrument books, videos, and DVDs for seven major publishers. This library of instructional material, which teaches jazz, rock, bluegrass, country, and blues guitar, banjo, Dobro, and mandolin, is sold on six continents. He also teaches musical seminars on the west coast and has written for (and has been written about in) numerous guitar and banjo magazines. A jazz CD, a jazz performance DVD, and a bluegrass CD that showcase Sokolow's technique all received excellent reviews in the US and Europe.

If you think Sokolow still isn't versatile enough, know that he accompanied a Russian balalaika virtuoso at the swank Bonaventure Hotel in LA, won "The Gong Show," played lap steel on the "Tonight Show," picked Dobro with Chubby Checker, played mandolin with Rick James, and was the official banjo player for "The Survivor" TV show.

TIM EMMONS is an eclectic acoustic and electric bassist who has recorded and performed with many notable artists, including jazz artists Art Pepper, Eddie Harris, Tom Scott, David Benoit, Larry Carlton, Blue Mitchell, Joe Pass, and Herb Ellis. Tim has also played for pop, rock, and folk artists Rod Stewart, Bo Diddley, Judy Collins, Mary Wells, Martha Reeves, Maria Muldaur, Geoff Muldaur, Peter, Paul and Mary, and Ian Whitcomb; he has played bass for great singers such as Della Reese, Liza Minelli, Carol Channing, John Raitt, Linda Hopkins, Vikki Carr, Theodore Bikel, Shirley Jones, and Donna Summer.

Tim has toured the USA, Europe, Asia, and Latin America playing everything from bluegrass with Richard Greene to swing with the Glenn Miller Orchestra, Cab Calloway, and the Nicolas Brothers, to classical-jazz-fusion with Freeflight. He has also played on more than 100 film and television scores, including *The Incredibles*, *The Day After Tomorrow*, *The Negotiator*, *Something's Gotta Give*, *The Wedding Planner*, "The Simpsons," "Family Guy," "Dawson's Creek," and *Ren and Stimpy's Xmas Special*. Album credits include Stevie Wonder and Beyoncé, Josh Groban, Justin Timberlake, Brandy, Toni Braxton, Andrea Bocelli, Rufus Wainwright, Phantom Planet, Dru Hill, the Brooklyn Tabernacle Choir, and the "String Quartet Tribute" series for Linkin Park, Good Charlotte, the Grateful Dead, Toby Keith, and Chevelle. Tim and Fred Sokolow are often seen playing together in the jazz venues of Los Angeles.

HAL LEONARD BASS METHOD

METHOD BOOKS

by Ed Friedland

BOOK 1

Book 1 teaches: tuning; playing position; musical symbols; notes within the first five frets; common bass lines, patterns and rhythms; rhythms through eighth notes; playing tips and techniques; more than 100 great songs, riffs and examples; and more! The audio includes 44 full-band tracks for demonstration or play-along.
00695067 Book Only...............................$7.99
00695068 Book/Online Audio...............$12.99

BOOK 2

Book 2 continues where Book 1 left off and teaches: the box shape; moveable boxes; notes in fifth position; major and minor scales; the classic blues line; the shuffle rhythm; tablature; and more!
00695069 Book Only...............................$7.99
00695070 Book/Online Audio...............$12.99

BOOK 3

With the third book, progressing students will learn more great songs, riffs and examples; sixteenth notes; playing off chord symbols; slap and pop techniques; hammer-ons and pull-offs; playing different styles and grooves; and more.
00695071 Book Only...............................$7.99
00695072 Book/Online Audio...............$12.99

COMPOSITE

This money-saving edition contains Books 1, 2 and 3.
00695073 Book Only.............................$17.99
00695074 Book/Online Audio...............$24.99

DVD

Play your favorite songs in no time with this DVD! Covers: tuning, notes in first through third position, rhythms through eighth notes, fingerstyle and pick playing, 4/4 and 3/4 time, and more! Includes 6 full songs and on-screen music notation. 68 minutes.
00695849 DVD.....................................$19.95

BASS FOR KIDS

by Chad Johnson

Bass for Kids is a fun, easy course that teaches children to play bass guitar faster than ever before. Popular songs such as "Crazy Train," "Every Breath You Take," "A Hard Day's Night" and "Wild Thing" keep kids motivated, and the clean, simple page layouts ensure their attention remains focused on one concept at a time.
00696449 Book/Online Audio $12.99

REFERENCE BOOKS

BASS SCALE FINDER

by Chad Johnson

Learn to use the entire fretboard with the *Bass Scale Finder*. This book contains over 1,300 scale diagrams for the most important 17 scale types.
00695781 6" x 9" Edition.....................$7.99
00695778 9" x 12" Edition....................$7.99

BASS ARPEGGIO FINDER

by Chad Johnson

This extensive reference guide lays out over 1,300 arpeggio shapes. 28 different qualities are covered for each key, and each quality is presented in four different shapes.
00695817 6" x 9" Edition.....................$7.99
00695816 9" x 12" Edition....................$7.99

MUSIC THEORY FOR BASSISTS

by Sean Malone

Acclaimed bassist and composer Sean Malone will explain the written language of music, using easy-to-understand terms and concepts, diagrams, and much more. The audio provides 96 tracks of examples, demonstrations, and play-alongs.
00695756 Book/Online Audio $17.99

STYLE BOOKS

BASS LICKS

by Ed Friedland

This comprehensive supplement to any bass method will help students learn over 200 great bass licks, lines and grooves in many rhythmic styles. *Bass Licks* illustrates how simple melodic patterns can become the springboard for group improvisation or the foundation of a song.
00696035 Book/Online Audio $14.99

BASS LINES

by Matt Scharfglass

500 expertly written bass lines, riffs and fills in a wide variety of musical genres are included in this comprehensive collection to help players expand their bass vocabulary. The examples cover many tempos, keys and feels, and include easy bass lines for beginners on up to advanced riffs for more experienced bassists.
00148194 Book/Online Audio $19.99

BLUES BASS

by Ed Friedland

Learn to play studying the songs of B.B. King, Stevie Ray Vaughan, Muddy Waters, Albert King, the Allman Brothers, T-Bone Walker, and many more. Learn riffs from blues classics including: Born Under a Bad Sign • Hideaway • Hoochie Coochie Man • Killing Floor • Pride and Joy • Sweet Home Chicago • The Thrill Is Gone • and more.
00695870 Book/Online Audio $14.99

COUNTRY BASS

by Glenn Letsch

21 songs, including: Act Naturally • Boot Scootin' Boogie • Crazy • Honky Tonk Man • Love You Out Loud • Luckenbach, Texas (Back to the Basics of Love) • No One Else on Earth • Ring of Fire • Southern Nights • Streets of Bakersfield • Whose Bed Have Your Boots Been Under? • and more.
00695928 Book/Online Audio $17.99

FRETLESS BASS

by Chris Kringel

18 songs, including: Bad Love • Continuum • Even Flow • Everytime You Go Away • Hocus Pocus • I Could Die for You • Jelly Roll • King of Pain • Kiss of Life • Lady in Red • Tears in Heaven • Very Early • What I Am • White Room • more.
00695850...$19.99

FUNK BASS

by Chris Kringel

This is your complete guide to learning the basics of grooving and soloing funk bass. Songs include: Can't Stop • I'll Take You There • Let's Groove • Stay • What Is Hip • and more.
00695792 Book/Online Audio..............$22.99

R&B BASS

by Glenn Letsch

This book/audio pack uses actual classic R&B, Motown, soul and funk songs to teach you how to groove in the style of James Jamerson, Bootsy Collins, Bob Babbitt, and many others. The 19 songs include: For Once in My Life • Knock on Wood • Mustang Sally • Respect • Soul Man • Stand by Me • and more.
00695823 Book/Online Audio $17.99

ROCK BASS

by Sean Malone

This book/audio pack uses songs from a myriad of rock genres to teach the key elements of rock bass. Includes: Another One Bites the Dust • Beast of Burden • Money • Roxanne • Smells like Teen Spirit • and more.
00695801 Book/Online Audio..............$21.99

SUPPLEMENTARY SONGBOOKS

These great songbooks correlate with Books 1-3 of the *Hal Leonard Bass Method*, giving students great songs to play while they're still learning! The audio tracks include great accompaniment and demo tracks.

EASY POP BASS LINES

20 great songs that students in Book 1 can master. Includes: Come as You Are • Crossfire • Great Balls of Fire • Imagine • Surfin' U.S.A. • Takin' Care of Business • Wild Thing • and more.
00695810 Book Only.............................$9.99
00695809 Book/Online Audio..............$15.99

MORE EASY POP BASS LINES

20 great songs for Level 2 students. Includes: Bad, Bad Leroy Brown • Crazy Train • I Heard It Through the Grapevine • My Generation • Pride and Joy • Ramblin' Man • Summer of '69 • and more.
00695819 Book Only...........................$12.99
00695818 Book/Online Audio..............$16.99

EVEN MORE EASY POP BASS LINES

20 great songs for Level 3 students, including: ABC • Another One Bites the Dust • Brick House • Come Together • Higher Ground • Iron Man • The Joker • Sweet Emotion • Under Pressure • more.
00695821 Book.....................................$9.99
00695820 Book/Online Audio..............$16.99

Visit Hal Leonard online at
www.halleonard.com

Prices, contents and availability subject to change without notice.
Some products may not be available outside of U.S.A.